From

AUSCHWITZ

to

ALDERNEY

From

AUSCHWITZ

to

ALDERNEY

———

Tom Freeman-Keel

Dedicated to those
who died in the
cause of freedom

Published by
Seek Publishing,
P.O. Box 3,
Craven Arms
Shropshire
England
SY7 0WB

ISBN 0 9526912 0 5

Produced by Axxent Ltd
99-101, St Leonards Road, Windsor,
Berkshire, SL4 3BZ

CONTENTS

> The Author wishes to draw attention to the fact that the ideas propounded by him that the 'underground hospitals' in Jersey and Guernsey were intended for eventual conversion to gaschambers are not necessarily those of the contributors and persons mentioned in this book.

ACKNOWLEDGEMENTS

First, to that particular person who challenged me to write at all and for whom this book was written.

To Miss A. E. Preston without whose unfaltering encouragement, help and support this book may not have been finished.

And to my many friends who urged me on my way and to those friends in the Channel Islands who smoothed my path and were so helpful, with especial mention of Michael Ginns of the Channel Islands Occupation Society (Jersey); of the staff at the Guernsey Military underground hospital; of (Bob) R V Le Sueur; of Norman Le Brocq and Stella Perkins ... all of Jersey.

To Mr David Winnick MP; to the helpful staffs of the Imperial War Museum Library, the Board of Deputies of British Jews; the Institute of Contemporary History and Wiener Library Ltd; and the staff of Holywell Library who went beyond the call of duty in helping my research work.

To Evelyn Julia Kent author of 'Eva's Story' and to those radio commentators and journalists who had the faith to give me time and space in their media, and also Mrs Ann Griffiths (Ann Corkett) who loaned so much useful material.

But in particular to my four contributors ... Margaret Brockley; Joe Miere; Tommy Syms and Vassili Marempolski who so generously gave of their time and memories in preparing their Testimonies, not forgetting Nicholas Koral who so willingly and expertly translated from the Ukrainian.

In a book constructed of information available from such diverse sources it is possible, despite the efforts made, that some original owners of copyright may have been overlooked. The author's apologies are extended in such cases. Errors and omissions in text and acknowledgements will be corrected and published in future editions.

Attention is also drawn to the Contents page in which will be found a declaration that the opinions expressed in this book are those of the Author only.

PREFACE

How did I come to write this book?

I had always been fascinated by 'Mein Kampf'.

By rubbing shoulders with politicians as a journalist before the war I formed a number of opinions. They lay dormant for many years.

Then I lived in Jersey and saw the 'underground hospitals'. My curiosity was aroused for where ever I went my enquiries met a wall of silence.

In 1989 I heard of the rumoured list of 300,000 British for extinction had we lost the war. Again my enquiries and searches drew a blank.

Then I heard of the secret tapes, the 'Black Book' and the files held under the Secrets Act until the year 2045.

Since then I have, like a jig-saw, put the pieces together and this book is the picture I revealed.

To the uninitiated perhaps the most mind chilling thought is the employment by the Germans of architects, engineers and builders for the purpose of creating the machinery for the systematic, industrialised extermination of a whole race of people.

This was the cold blooded, calculated planning of people who knew what they were doing.

Perhaps the most frightening aspect of it all was the manner in which the evil reached into the hearts and minds of the masses, as typhus is carried on dust particles by the wind so was the cancer of genocide carried like an invisible cloud throughout the nation making it impossible to know whom had been affected.

Once beaten, France became infected ... remember the Concentration Camp in the centre of Paris!

It is not unreasonable to ask, if Russia and Britain had been beaten, if we too would have fallen under the evil spell of the Nazi doctrine. Some Russians and Ukrainians were already serving the Nazis and what of the Channel Islanders?

Where would the extermination of unwanted people have stopped?

Not just a few of Hitler's regime were involved, but the fabric of a whole nation. Influential, powerful people from all aspects of Society were prepared to 'join in'. Bankers, Entertainers, Artists, Industrialists, Inventors, Architects, Builders, Scientists closed their eyes to the meaning of the monster they were helping to create and were serving.

The same canker is working still today.

That was the picture the jig-saw revealed.

For whatever reason writers have ignored the subject of the possibility of gaschambers in the Channel Islands and the Final Solution brought to Britain perhaps because in doing so some unpalatable truths about our rulers at the time of the Second World War would be revealed.

The truth is a hard taskmaster to serve, and one of those truths is that we have learned nothing which has lessened mankind's inhumanity to man. It is only necessary to contemplate events in Bosnia, Rwanda and other places all over the world.

Churchill prefaced his *'History of the Second World War'* with these words

'In war: resolution

In defeat: defiance

In victory: magnanimity

In peace: goodwill.

Was he right? Should he not have written 'In peace, goodwill with caution'?

How often must a Rotweiller dog bite you before you muzzle it? Or perhaps put it in a kennel on a lead?

The contribution by the German race to the knowledge of the civilised world in Science, Art, Music, History and Philosophy has been outstanding, but the German nation also has a long history of aggression and has been responsible for two world wars. We should never forget, and never permit those who follow us, to forget either.

It would seem that we **have** forgotten for before us is unfolding in the newspapers and on television a scenario of weak Governments and appeasement almost identical to that which preceded World War II.

This latest 'Rotweiller' is a 'dog' sired by World War II, and a great play is being enacted of labelling President Milosevic and General Ratko Mladic as war criminals. But, we can be sure they will never appear before an International Court.

The new Court is without teeth. Laws forbid the deportation of war criminals for trial in The Hague providing the alleged war criminals remain within the boundaries of their own countries. This same law which has been operational in Germany since soon after the war has prevented the British from bringing to justice known war criminals of World War II still living in Germany who committed atrocities in Alderney.

There is a failure in the thinking of the British ruling classes and hierarchy to recognise a fundamental difference in the thinking processes of the German from our own, a thesis which is well developed in Chapter XIX 'The Germans' in Ralph Durand's book 'Guernsey under German Rule'.

So ... Peace and Goodwill with caution ...

As a Mayor of Dublin said in a speech on 10th July 1790 ...

"The condition upon which God hath given liberty to Man is eternal vigilance".

I hope this book will contribute towards that 'vigilance'.

Tom Freeman-Keel

LIST OF ILLUSTRATIONS

In order of appearance in the book

Front Cover:
Commandant SS-Sturmbahnfuhrer Maximilian List, head of the Sylt SS Concentration Camp in Alderney. In the background: prisoners' graveyard on Longy Common, Alderney. By courtesy of 'The Mail on Sunday'

EVENTFUL DATES IN THE OCCUPATION OF THE CHANNEL ISLANDS

1940	June 15	Demilitarisation of the Islands decided upon
	16-20	Evacuation of the Military
	17-19	Evacuation of St Malo by the Channel Islands small boats
	19	Islanders told to evacuate their Islands on an ad-hoc basis
	21-23	Panic evacuation of 30,000 Islanders
	28	Germans bomb and strafe all three Islands killing 40 people
	30	Occupation of Guernsey
	July 1	Germans occupy Jersey
	2	Alderney occupied
	Sept 27	Anti-Semitic Laws introduced
1941	Mar 17	François Scornet executed
	21	Sabotage denounced by Carey the Guernsey Bailiff
	June 15	Hitler orders fortification of the Islands
	July 8	£25 reward offered to informers by Carey for information on V-Victory signs
	Oct 13	Mrs Winifred Green imprisoned in Caen
	20	Hitler issues another Directive concerning Fortifications
	Apr 6	German begins to be taught in primary schools
1942	June 26	All wirelesses required to be handed in
	Sept 16/18 & 29	2073 non-Islanders deported to Germany from the three Islands

xv

	Oct 12	14 young men court-martialled for protesting about deportations
1943	Jan 18	German made compulsory in schools
	Feb 23	Sylt concentration camp established
	Mar 1	Kommandant SS Colonel Maximilian List is appointed Sylt camp commandant
	3	Conscription of Island Labour is illegally instituted
	June 22	Mrs Louisa Gould and Harold Le Druillenec sentenced
1944	June 17	Hitler orders German Forces must defend Islands 'to the last'
	July	Camp inmates moved to St Malo and Buchenwald
	Sept 9	Gas supply ceases in Jersey
	25	Chief of Staff von Helldorf is replaced by Vice-Admiral Friedrich Huffmeier
	Nov 5-7	Red Cross supplies arranged for the Islanders
	Dec 21	Gas supply ceases in Guernsey
	Dec 27	Red Cross ship Vega arrives for the first time
1945	Jan 12	End of telephone service
	25	End of electricity supply
	Mar 25	Huffmeier declares 'no surrender'
	28	Communal cafes and kitchens closed
	May 9	Jersey and Guernsey liberated
	16	Alderney liberated

BACKGROUND

For those who lived through the dark days of Occupation of the Channel Islands by the Germans there remains memories of events over which a question mark still hangs. Four of those survivors are contributors to this book, their testimonies, which have never been told before, underline what some Islanders, journalists and historians, have suspected since the day of liberation.

Mrs Margaret Brockley, then Miss James, was six when the German Forces arrived in 1940, and when Mr Vassili Marempolski arrived as a prisoner from the Ukraine he was only fifteen. Tommy Syms was ten when he was deported to Biberach and Joe Miere seventeen when sent to prison for seven months for resistance.

It is only in recent years, with the release of previously classified documents held in the Guernsey archives since 1945 that the extent of the horrors and atrocities which occurred in the Islands have been revealed.

These documents, classified, 'official', 'personally sensitive', 'secret', and 'not to be released until 2045', have been the source of a great deal of curiosity and speculation.

An official history had been written and published in 1975. Titled 'The German Occupation of the Channel Islands' by the late Dr. Charles Cruickshank, the book runs to a total of 370 pages but fails to mention the 'secret' documents in the Guernsey archives, to which, in view of the absence of information, now available, even he was apparently given only limited access.

Dr. Cruickshank's handling of the detail is faultless in that he records facts as they were revealed to him and were recorded by Major Pantcheff the British Intelligence Officer sent by the War Office after liberation, to investigate

1

allegations of brutality and mass murder. The sad fact is that Major Pantcheff's report was inaccurate.

However impersonal Dr. Cruickshank attempted to be he could not resist the temptation to palliate this damning record by stating 'At their face value they (the records) suggest that the Germans in Alderney were less callous than has been believed'.

The records to which he refers of course are those kept by the SS and the Todt Organisation first commanded by Colonel Maximilian List under whom worked Kurt Klebeck and Karl Theiss.

List and Klebeck were disciplined for incompetence when a number of Alderney prisoners destined for the Neuengamme death camp escaped and 50 died on the journey causing corpse disposal problems.

Klebeck was later taken from Alderney and sent to the Russian front where he committed further atrocities for which he was sentenced by a British Military Court in 1947, to 10 years imprisonment. (See the Attorney General's reply to Mr. David Winnick's question of Monday 11th May 1992, page 64).

It had been common knowledge since before 1945 that the most appalling atrocities had been committed in Alderney by all three camp commandants.

All three were allowed to escape and not one of them has been brought to justice for what happened in Alderney.

Interest has largely centered upon Kurt Klebeck for it was he who is alleged to have been responsible for 350 deaths in Alderney.

Contrary to Mr. Peter King's assumption in his book 'The Channel Islands War', Klebeck did not die and is still at large in Germany.

In 1992 out of a total of 33 files in the Guernsey archives 26 were reluctantly released. These files had originally been scheduled for retention until the year 2045

The reason for release was the growing pressure upon the Government by Members of Parliament and the media for more information upon the atrocities allegedly committed in

Alderney by Nazi Authorities and the alleged co-operation offered to them by Guernsey Authorities.

Foremost in the move was the Labour Member of Parliament, David Winnick supported by 30 other MPs. Also active was the 'All Party Parliamentary War Crimes Group'.

For over a year Mr. Winnick put pressure upon the Prime Minister, the Home Office, the Ministry of Defence, the Attorney General, the Germany Embassy and the Bailiff of Jersey. These documents were eventually released in November 1992 but there was a sting in the tail for **it was revealed that out of the 26 files 'released' 16 of them had suffered 'extraction' for reasons either of 'national security' or 'personal sensitivity'.**

Of the remaining seven files Mr. Kenneth Clarke MP. QC. offered the reason for extended closure under (section 5(1) of the Public Record Act 1958 on the grounds of 'personal sensitivity' (see page 73).

But this reason was contradicted in a letter to Mr. Winnick from The Viscount Cranborne, then Parliamentary Under-Secretary of State for Defence on 17th February 1993 in which he says 'contrary to media reports, they were not part of the War Office's post-liberation war crimes investigations', but 'concerned debriefing by the Military Intelligence' requiring military intelligence from men who had visited Guernsey and returned with information.

Who is attempting to fool whom?

With the outstanding changes in technological warfare in recent years what possible importance can there be in 'military information' 50 years old, let alone 100 years old? As, in 1940, the British Military had designated the Channel Islands as 'of no particular military importance' (a view shared by the German High Command but not Hitler) what possible importance can the Islands be in any future conflict?

Surely, only the most sensitive of records can justifiably be withheld from public scrutiny for such a long period?

The reason for the retention of the seven files could be interpreted in many ways. Was it a ploy to divert attention from the fact that of the 26 files released 16 had been 'tampered with' by the Home Office and the Ministry of Defence? If so, then it failed, for Mr. Winnick was quick to point out in a letter (see page 76) to Mr. Kenneth Clarke QC. MP., then Secretary of State for the Home Department that 'there does not seem to be amongst the released documents any relating to the camps on Alderney'.

The result of the 'extractions' of course was to make the 26 files innocuous.

The questions raised by Mr. Winnick were concerned with a German, now resident in Germany, who could only be tried in Germany. If, as it seems, the Government were not anxious to pursue this line of attack by submitting the relevant documents of proof to the German Authorities, it was necessary only to withhold documents on grounds of 'secrecy'.

Whilst the War Crimes Act had been passed many years previously, no one it seemed, wished to use its powers to find and bring to justice a number of War Criminals still free and sheltering in this country. The reluctance of the British Government to take action it seems, is comparable with that of the Germans. (see pages 63,64,85,71,79).

It should be noted here in defence of the German Public Prosecutor of Hamburg that he requested from the British Ministry of Defence in November 1992 the relevant documents to enable him to proceed with investigations. The Ministry of Defence finally replied in May 1993! Six months later!

As the papers relevant to committal of Kurt Klebeck were only released to Germany in 1993 what papers were sent to the USSR in 1945 to assist them in connection with convicting the same man? Is it of any wonder that the USSR did nothing?

Was the purpose of this action to protect the families of those Channel Island Officials who had been accused by others of too willing collaboration during the Occupation of Guernsey?

Perhaps the seven files revealed the strength of the anti-semitic sympathies which existed then, both in the Channel Isles and in Britain.

Or did they reveal a knowledge of the true purpose of the 'underground hospitals' long suspected by some as for eventual conversion to gas-chambers? Any suggestion that this latter was so has been stoutly refuted, yet 'hospitals' as places of sinister purpose had been revealed as long ago as 1945 in the film shot by the late Lord Sidney Bernstein on the order of the British Government as a record of war time atrocities committed by the Nazis.

More about the film will be found in this book but sufficient to say that having ordered the making of the film, when reviewed by the Department of Propaganda and other controlling bodies it was considered too horrific for general release.

Before the extraction of some of the content from the 26 files released, they were expected to disclose atrocities committed in the Channel Islands of Alderney comparable with any committed by the Germans elsewhere. We still do not have documentary proof.

Whilst the demands of the curious and the suspicious have, to a degree, been met, it has also served to whet the appetite of others.

In fact, speculation as to what went on in Guernsey and in Alderney has not been allayed but inflamed. Such questions, in addition to those relating to ill-treatment of prisoners working in Guernsey by Guernsey collaborators and the alleged too eager collaboration of the Authorities with the German Occupying Forces are now supplemented by suggestions of incompetence or deliberate rejection or omission of evidence, by the investigating Military and Civil Authorities who visited Guernsey in 1945.

Fraud, on a large scale committed with the connivance of the German and the British Authorities has also been suggested.

It seems that only the release of the whole contents of all 33 files will quieten such suspicions.

Such release it is hoped will help to make the trial of Kurt Klebeck a possibility.

By mid- 1995 it will be almost 3 years since questions regarding atrocities and 'strange happenings' in the Channel Islands, were first raised.

The most likely reason for the continued retention of the files is the protection of the families of those Channel Island Officials who had been accused by others of too willing collaboration during the Occupation.

The retention however has the effect of keeping the reputation of some who might well have been innocent still under suspicion and for their sakes a total release is surely required?

An incident, which might have no more significance than that of an ordinary burglary yet in the circumstances, might be equally suspicious, was the theft in 1991 of files concerning the Occupation from the Archives in Jersey.

The files at the time were not considered of sufficient importance to be kept under strict guard.

Most of the files were soon recovered by the Jersey Police and two persons were convicted of theft. The remainder of the files have now been recovered and are now with the newly created Jersey Archives Service, but they were in the hands of thieves sufficiently long for them to be copied.

Whilst the thieves were caught, tried and convicted the Jersey Police, evidently satisfied, closed the files, taking no further action against people who had previously been under suspicion.

It is tempting to ask what could have been in those files? Why were they not in safe keeping? What was so important that someone wished to remove them before they became public knowledge? And were they copied before being retrieved? Where are the copies now?

It is interesting to note that whereas what is left of the files are now, in proper circumstances, available for scrutiny only some of the files in Guernsey can be seen.

Only since the demands for the release of such files have become irresistable have the States of Jersey – 50 years since the end of the war – decided to set up an Archivist Service.

The retention of the remaining documents in Guernsey, not to be released until 2045, seems only to have inflamed suspicions that something sinister occurred which both Island States and Whitehall do not want disclosed until everyone is dead and the living will have lost interest.

That the Islanders suffered the most incredible hardships, increasingly with each year of the occupation, there is no doubt. In fact their suffering began before the Germans arrived, largely due to the inefficiency of the various departments in Whitehall and their inability to appreciate the gravity and urgency of the situation. The Home Office and the War Office were in conflict.

It had been alleged that right up to the outbreak of war holidaymakers were arriving in the Channel Islands. Some, unable to make their getaway became caught up in the Occupation and eventually found themselves in concentration camps on the Continent.

For weeks the Bailiff of Jersey was left uninformed as to what was going on in Whitehall. He received no directives on what to do about the demilitarisation of his Island. Never the less according to a pre-arranged plan he acted in every way that was expected of him. Apparently Whitehall found the situation more difficult to encompass.

When finally troops and Island Militia were removed from the Island in a hurry the civilian population caught the fever and panicked. The saga of the evacuation of Guernsey and Alderney is one of unmitigated panic and inefficiency.

Eventually almost half the population left the Island before the arrival of the Germans.

In Jersey the evacuation was more orderly and only one fifth of the population decided to leave.

The official boats supposedly despatched from England had not arrived. In order to meet the thousands of panicking islanders who had swept down to the quays coal boats, potato boats and whatever seagoing vessels were available were pressed into service. Many of them were unsuitable for the hazardous journey ahead.

Without food and water and proper sanitation some of them set off across what is well known to the regular sailor as 'a nasty piece of water'. Some took more than 24 hours to reach England.

There must, in the minds of many true Islanders (some of whom had never felt anything more that a partial fidelity towards Great Britain) have been doubts as to where their loyalties might lie.

If the lawyers of the United Kingdom and the Channel Island States, when faced with the first great constitutional crisis for 800 years could not make up their minds about the exact status of the Channel Isles, it was understandable that the general population would also wonder what next to do.

Channel Islanders had lived in a state of delightful isolation and confident security for so long, any suggestion, if made only six months earlier, that the situation could disintegrate over night would have been beyond their comprehension.

The paradise which they had so jealously guarded was about to vanish. Personal feelings of self-preservation would, as with most, override any high minded moral attitudes of national loyalty, at least for a time.

The reader who hopes to find detailed descriptions and accounts of the long drawn out, confusing and sometimes conflicting exchanges between the various Government Departments of the United Kingdom and the States of Jersey and Guernsey, which preceded the outbreak of the war and subsequent Occupation by the Germans will look in vain.

Much has been written about this already in great detail by Dr. Charles Cruickshank and Mr. Peter King in their books. There are many other good informative books on the same subject. But the first hand accounts by Margaret Brockley, Tommy Syms and Vassili Marempolski contained in this book are told for the first time.

Incidents of unbelievable selfish behaviour, of neighbour spying and reporting, of excessive collaboration have been cited. It can only be hoped they were not common. The community was under great stress. The very geographical position of the Islands precluded the population from becoming 'refugees' in the context in which we have come to understand the word in recent years in countries throughout the world.

The Islands' Authorities, having been informed, after months of legal confusion and administrative indecision, that they would be abandoned by Britain until the Nazis had been defeated, were faced with a prospect hardly likely to cheer the hearts of any.

The 1500 occupants of Alderney had lived on a see-saw of administrative indecision for days as to whether Alderney would be totally evacuated, and, in fact the evacuation of Guernsey had already commenced before the order was given that everyone in Alderney must leave. These hapless people had little more than 24 hours notice. Such was the haste that some left half finished meals on tables and left front doors ajar. Two were to remain.

The reader expecting to find detailed accounts of the sufferings of the Islanders will look in vain. Details of the rationing and the food shortages; the black market which arose over night will be found in other books, for it is of the stuff of all civil populations of a conquered nation overrun by a victorious army.

During the first year there was a state of more or less peaceful co-existence with the Germans providing everyone behaved themselves.

A Resistance Movement, such as had operated with some success in France and Yugoslavia, could not have survived in the Channel Islands. There was no room to manoeuvre – no place to hide.

Certainly the residents of these small islands must have felt the sense of being trapped without means of escape. Accounts recorded elsewhere might be those of a people anywhere in Europe under the Nazi Jackboot.

The few attempts at spying, sabotage and even accidental insult to the German forces were dealt with harshly.

When the British carried out a number of petty raiding operations for the purpose of obtaining information, reprisals followed. The raiders were discovered by the Germans or disclosed by the Islanders themselves trying to avoid reprisals.

All of these 'military excursions' vividly described in Dr. Cruickshank's book were only partly effective or were abortive with the exception of one. It is this single exception about which a question is raised later in this book.

It is of course not known whether the British Military, in making these raids seriously questioned what the effect would be upon the population.

More than a dozen plans were prepared for the invasion of, or for 'sorties' into, the various Islands, but were abandoned.

A large-scale invasion of the Islands, to be called 'Attaboy' was seriously considered by Sir Winston Churchill and Lord Mountbatten. They differed on how it should be carried out. Each seemed to be vying with the other to produce a 'master plan' of military achievement, in what at best, was only a small area in the theatre of war and when available military resources were at their very lowest.

The problem of whether, and how, to attack was considered by the Military Command in England and this is adequately covered by Dr. Cruickshank's book. Suffice it to say that the idea was abandoned very early in the war.

Why, when opposed by the professionals, did Churchill and Mountbatten still toy with the idea of going ahead? Having spent weeks before war was declared trying to decide whether to defend or abandon the Islands, and finally, in a hurry, evacuated the military and some of the population, it should have been reconsidered, is beyond comprehension. Without the reoccupation of Jersey and Guernsey an invasion of Alderney would have been pointless and surely unsuccessful.

It was fortunate that the heads of the different Commands of Air, Sea and Land were in unison and adamant in opposing the crazy plans for assault on Alderney. Finally Winston Churchill decided 'No', but the impetuous, flamboyant, self seeking Lord Mountbatten persisted.

British Intelligence must have been poorly informed of the hundreds of Guernsey workers who had been drafted back into Alderney. Or did Mountbatten pay no heed to this fact?

The Germans were in control of the Guernsey and Jersey airports and huge long range guns had been installed in Guernsey, which, if turned upon Alderney, could easily have totally destroyed the Island.

If all this was due to lack of intelligence, why it may be reasonable to ask, did not British Military Intelligence see to it that a secret communication centre was established before the Islands were abandoned to the Germans?

The reader might well ask "then what is there left to tell?"

What is left to tell is what should have been understood and anticipated after a careful study of *Mein Kampf* and German Nazi behaviour in the decade prior to the outbreak of war.

Once the Germans had arrived notices soon appeared stating that any form of sabotage or resistance would bring down retribution on the general public. One young man seventeen years old was imprisoned for months for a very minor act of 'obstruction' and our contributor, Mrs Brockley, then only eight years old, was taken to SS Headquarters and interrogated for hours because she accidentally dropped a cherry pip on the cap of a passing Officer.

Whilst the Islanders undoubtedly suffered the most incredible hardships increasing with each year of the Occupation, a reasonably peaceful form of co-existence was established.

Islanders were to see what remained of the few able bodied young men deported to prisoner of war camps, in France and Germany. The few Jews who remained on the Islands were first persecuted and then deported to concentration camps, probably Auschwitz, for all but two never returned and finally all those people on the Islands who could not claim to be of true Jersey or Guernsey origination were sent to camps in France and Germany.

Altogether, thousands were deported to the continent. **It is not difficult to see in all this 'the shape of things to come' had the Nazis achieved victory over Britain.**

The Nazis were of course aware of a small hard-core of strong sympathisers in Britain. They were also aware of a much larger group of potential sympathisers in the upper echelons of society who might be easily won over providing the ruthless side of the Nazi administration was kept out of sight and out of knowing.

This is where the usefulness of the Channel Islands, once the war was won for the Nazis, would become evident.

The contemplation of what would have followed a Nazi victory is horrific. Is this what is being kept within the 'secret' files until 2045? Or, is somewhere hidden in those seven files, a list of influential names who might have turned happily co-operative?

In 1945, in the archives of the SS, British Military Intelligence discovered a list of 2820 persons who were to be taken into custody immediately upon a Nazi victory.

The list 'Sonderfahndungsliste G.B.' is better known as the 'Black Book' and is available for public examination. Its existence was kept secret until 1985.

As the list of those whom Nazis would have arrested, imprisoned and presumably executed, was already known and available it would be naive to suppose they did not also have a list of potential collaborators.

So... what is left is one of the most frightening 'might have been' speculations of Word War II.

In the early days of America's war with Japan things did not go well and throughout the world Britain's survival and fate balanced on a knife edge. Japan had already reached the Indian/Burmese border. Had Britain capitulated to the Germans there is little doubt the British campaign in Burma and the Far East would have been stopped at the demand of Germany.

Japan would have overrun India and very soon the British Forces in North Africa, fighting on two fronts, must have capitulated thus permitting the Germans and Japanese to meet in the Middle East.

Germany, now with a free hand and occupying the British Isles would have dropped her mantle of appeasement and co-operation and the British Holocaust.... the murder of hundreds of thousands of British subjects – would have begun.

This book presents powerful circumstantial evidence that the 450,000 Jews in Britain of British, German and Central European origin would have been exterminated and with them 2820 of the most notable anti-Nazi figures, commencing, of course, with Sir Winston Churchill. (He is in the *Black Book*).

As the disposal of such vast numbers without offending the susceptibilities of the pro-Nazi/anti-semitic group within the Establishment might prove a problem, the 'underground hospitals' in the Channel Islands had been prepared for conversion into gaschambers.

Alderney had already been organised as a group of concentration camps for prisoners from all over Europe to be used as labourers on the defence works.

It is left to anyone to speculate as to whether Winston Churchill paused to contemplate such a scenario.

He was, despite his appointment as Prime Minister, fighting a battle on two fronts, one of which the majority of the British public were totally unaware.

The menace of the Germans and the Japanese everyone understood but few realised the opposition which had preceded Winston Churchill's appointment as Prime Minister and which continued even **after** his appointment.

Winston Churchill suffered a barrage of criticism and petty obstructions from a substantial part of the Tory benches, the Lords and the Establishment, encouraged it is alleged, by the King and Queen.

Britain was in peril, but the political infighting continued oblivious of the peril. Only Winston Churchill, supported by Lord Beaverbrook, Brendan Bracken and others stood firm and resolute.

Did Churchill, just once say to himself a line of Kipling's 'If'...

> *'If you can keep your head when all about you*
> *are losing their's and blaming it on you'.*

Whilst this was going on in London, in Guernsey, a tableau of what was in store for Britain was being enacted.

ଔଓ

But would strong leadership have been enough?

The strong leadership of Mr Winston Churchill, as he then was, is sometimes considered to be the reason why Britain and her Allies won the war. The thought that despite his leadership we would have lost is too disagreeable, for many, to contemplate. Never-the-less there is no doubt that had Hitler decided to invade immediately after Dunkirk, following the devastation of the British Expeditionary Forces, when we had nothing to fight back with, he would have succeeded.

American Government, at this stage, did not want to become involved. Infact there was a strong pro-Hitler lobby and a well established Nazi Organisation.

There had been no Pearl Harbour.

The USSR/German non-agression pact was still in place.

The stage was set for German victory in Britain.

In fact, it was only the apparently incomprehensible decision of Hitler to attack the USSR instead of Britain, which saved us. There are a few who would say it was not the British nor the Americans who won the war, but the Russians, not because they wanted to fight but because Hitler forced them to do so.

It was, some say his greatest mistake. **But was it?**

Yet on reflection, it was the obvious action to take:- Hitler could not, whilst attacking Britain afford to expose his Eastern Front (the pact was a sham and Russia would have attacked). He needed the oil and the manpower of the captured Russian Armies and civilians as a work force.

He also knew the British and the U.S.A. were as nervous of the USSR as they were of his own ambitions.

With the defeat and elimination of the Communist threat to the West Hitler was confident of co-operation from Britain, and a benign attitude from the U.S.A.

So far as the Channel Islands are concerned, out of the mass of material in records, books and interviews with eye witnesses, a few basic details bearing more than an element of truth have emerged.

1) That, on September 1st 1939 at the outbreak of war the Channel Island States moved quickly and efficiently, carrying out what was expected of them. On contacting the British Government they were told 'not to worry'. Days passed. Nothing was heard from Whitehall.

2) That, when it became obvious the Channel Isles could not be defended and demilitarisation and evacuation was necessary, the British Government and Military and Civil Authorities were slow, inefficient, indecisive and muddled

and failed properly to respond to the cries for help from the Channel Island States.

3) That, having agreed to demilitarisation and having assisted the Channel Island States in that exercise, the British Government forgot to inform the German High Command the Islands had been demilitarised with the result the Islands were bombed.

4) That, the British Military were slow in organising the evacuation vessels for the Islands, resulting in the Channel Island States, because of the ensuing panic, having to organise makeshift plans.

5) That, in the opinion of many, from the beginning, and right through to the end, the States Authorities, particularly Guernsey, were considered to have been unnecessarily co-operative with Nazis.

6) That, the States Authorities in both Islands collaborated with the Germans in organising the deportation of more than 2000 of the Islands' civil inhabitants. Almost all were English nationals or Jews, finishing up in concentration camps, Auschwitz and other death camps. Some returned others did not.

7) That the War Department organised a number of petty, abortive attempts, at information-gathering sorties, all but one of which failed or were mostly ineffective.

8) That, for 11 months following D Day the Channel Isles were ignored and left in the hands of the German Forces before liberation occurred, thus giving ample time for the Nazis to destroy evidence. During this period the inhabitants, both German and civil came near to starvation.

9) That, at least three of the Germans who should have been brought to trial for atrocities committed in Alderney are still at large.

10) That many Jersey people and some Guernsey People also, in so far as they were able, and in many cases well beyond

the call of duty, carried out acts of resistance throughout the war.

11) That the blanket of secrecy regarding 'happenings' in the Islands, particularly in Guernsey and Alderney, has not been lifted, despite strong protestations from the British Government that it has.

THE REVELATIONS

During the Christmas of 1937/8, when the world trembled on the brink of war and Chamberlain, who had never read 'Mein Kampf', returned waving a useless piece of paper, a young woman teacher, known to the Author, with a bright spirit of adventure and no political awareness made the journey to Munich to visit a German pen friend, a young male fellow teacher.

A handsome young German, also travelling to Munich in the same carriage, politely offered his companionship to alleviate the boredom. He asked questions about English politics and about Britain.

When it got dark the young woman lay down to sleep. It was cold. The young German gallantly covered her with his coat.

As dawn was breaking the young man awoke the girl. He was blowing on the frosted window – making a hole to see through. He beckoned her over, and pointing, said 'look'...'look' 'that's Dachau ... it is the finest prison in the world – the most modern'.

The teacher, sleepy bemused and not understanding what he was talking about, saw only fences, high walls, barbed wire, as they flashed past.

When they arrived in Munich and she had met her friend, the young man of the train invited them to his home, where he took them to his room and proudly displayed his 'Brown Shirt' Nazi uniform.

The teacher's innocence regarding Dachau is forgivable and understandable, but to suggest, as was maintained after the war by British Authorities that nothing was known about Dachau and the other Camps must be nonsense.

Other nations too had turned an equally blind eye, yet the Germans themselves had, during the preceding six years, made no secret of Dachau publicly expressing pride in what they claimed was the finest of all prisons.

Dachau was not the only concentration camp, some 50 had already been established throughout Germany before 1938.

Following the outbreak of war in 1939 Dachau was used by the SS doctors for medical experiments on prisoners, particularly Jews and Russian prisoners.

Experiments included submerging prisoners in icy water until they lost consciousness and thereafter testing the state of the blood as the body temperature dropped.

Some prisoners were used for experiments with only salt water to drink and no food to eat. Others were used to test the effect of rapid variations in air pressure as a guide to what happened in high altitude and parachute descents from great heights. Women were subject to unspeakable experiments and forced pregnancy.

It was also a concentration camp for priests of whom 2800 were admitted between 1940 and 1945, nearly all of whom died there, mainly from typhus.

The German commandant Weiss and 39 co-defendants were found guilty and executed on charges of atrocities by an American military court in December 1945.

Dachau is a little village only 10 miles from Munich.

Before the First World War Hitler had moved to Munich. He liked Munich. He had enlisted there, and following having been wounded was in hospital in Munich. Munich seemed to have a special place in his life.

For his part in the failed uprising in 1923 he was imprisoned in Landsberg castle where he wrote 'Mein Kampf', the book which was to become the Nazi bible. Released within a year he set about rebuilding the National Socialist party and in the course of its development The Brown House in Munich became the headquarters and the Brown Shirts were born.

To say, as has been suggested from time to time in defence of Hitler that he knew nothing of the atrocities being perpetrated in Dachau is of course nonsense.

Reference to some of the notes from 'Mein Kampf' at the back of this book will dispel such doubts.

For example there is Egon Hansfatsengel's story told during an interview ...

"We knew as schoolboys about Dachau ... there was a ditty which we all repeated, including people, who later disclaimed all knowledge of that sort of thing ... and the ditty went ...

"Dear God, strike me dumb, so
that I shan't be sent to Dachau".

If a schoolboy knew of such things and the Hitler Youth then why not Hitler?

That the inmates of these notorious camps were mostly Jews and that most Germans were willing to ignore Jewish persecution, and, perhaps welcome what was going on around them, was a lesson learned by the Nazis long before the war and was exploited by them during the war and put to the test with good results during their occupation of the Channel Islands.

In England, in the years prior to the war, teachers, farm-workers, factory workers and bus-drivers, starved of information, could be forgiven for being unaware of what was going on in Germany. It is difficult to accept that the inmates of the famous Clubs, the Military and the Politicians did **not** know.

Elsewhere in this book appears a list of pro-Nazi, anti-semitic sympathisers active **before** the war and during the war. To suppose that they would not have known, and would not have discussed events in Germany, where ever they may have met, is stretching credulity to the limit.

Political Intelligence Departments of all Western Nations, including the British treated reports with scepticism and the British continued to do so after the war even when confronted with irrefutable evidence.

21

In European countries before the war not yet under the Nazi Jackboot the fear of political terrorism and of the Informer had not been felt and people were therefore able, with the information available to make their own judgements, draw their conclusions, and discuss them openly.

The effect upon the ordinary person (as it is vividly told in Mrs. Brockley's testimony) once political terrorism has gripped the community is very different and is well illustrated in Emmi Bonhöffer's story as a survivor of a Concentration Camp.

"It was in '41 or '42, I was standing in the row in a shop, maybe 50 or 60 people were standing around me, and I told my neighbours; "Now they begin to kill the Jews in the concentration camps and burn them". And the shopkeeper, who had heard it, said: "If you do not stop telling such fairy tales you will end in the concentration camp, and nobody can help you, because every-one heard it". And I said "Well it's the truth and I feel you should know it". When I came home I told my husband, proud of my courage and he said... "You are absolutely crazy. Please understand, a dictatorship is like a snake, if you put your feet on its tail – and that is what you are doing – it will just bite you. You have to meet the head. And that's what you cannot do. Only the military can do it. They have the arms and they can get to him. Therefore the only thing which makes sense for resistance is to convince generals that they have to act".

The infamous 'Black Book' with its list of 2820 British nationals who were for extermination cannot be denied. Some extracts appear in this book. But even this was not made public until 1989. Found in SS Archives after the war it is difficult to accept that other equally interesting records were not discovered. Again the question is asked 'why did it take 44 years before the book was made public?'.

It is equally unbelievable that, even today, we are still expected by various Government Departments concerned and the Military, to discount the possibility that some 450,000 Jews residing in Britain would have suffered the same fate as the

4,000,000 who passed through Auschwitz, had Britain lost the war.

This attitude is not new for precisely the same posture of disbelief was expressed by similar people in the same Departments over 50 years ago when told of the German Camps.

The rumour which has persisted since 1945 that there were 300,000 for extermination and some 400 Irish nationals was inaccurate in its figures but was almost certainly true in its substance, some 450,000... not a mere 300,000... would have died.

By the end of the war some 5000 camps had been established throughout the occupied areas of Europe. Of these some 300 were destined to become 'gas' camps or were actually already operating as such. The most famous of these was Auschwitz/Birkenau. Belsen became one of the most notorious for the experiments carried out there on the inmates and where the prisoners were simply burned or left for dead. Other camps were at Biberach-an-der-Riss, Laufen, Spergau, Neuengaumme, Mauthausen, Ravensburg, Naumburg, Wilhelmshaven, Buchenwald and Wolfenbüttel.

Perhaps it is too much to expect that a clerk working in one of the 'Official sources of Information' in Whitehall in 1994, in response to a letter of enquiry should reply 'I have never heard of a list of 300,000 names for extermination and think it rather unlikely that such a document existed, given that such large numbers were not executed following the German seizure of France, Belgium and the Netherlands'.

Has the gentleman never heard of the trainloads which were shipped back into Germany from those countries? He has obviously not seen Sir Sidney Bernstein's film of the Concentration Camps in which Mr. Leon Greenman testifies to having been taken from Holland with his family to Auschwitz.

He saw his entire family being led away to be gassed and burned.

He survived.

It is a sad reflection that even within the Departments dealing with these subjects there should be such ignorance of the events of those times.

Does it, perhaps, highlight the ignorance of the 'better educated' or is it a wish not to be reminded of them. Or an example of the paranoia?

During the War Crimes Trials there were frequent attempts by some of the accused to excuse themselves by saying 'they were only obeying orders' or 'I was only part of it and did not realise the full implications of my actions'.

These excuses were only an extension of the remarks made by many of the German population when the war had ended. In Sidney Bernstein's film he recounts meetings with Mayors and Burgomasters of villages only the distance of a football pitch away from the barbed wire fencing of some of these camps who persisted in declaiming their ignorance of what was going on.

There would appear to have been little difference in the attitudes adopted by some of the Authorities in the Channel Isles once occupation had occurred, especially in Guernsey.

Yet within two of the testimonies appearing in this book it is made clear that the ordinary inhabitants of one Channel Island were almost totally ignorant of what was going on in the other, once Occupying Forces had imposed curfews and restrictions on movement.

A proper appreciation of these facts is important to the understanding of the argument that it would have been possible for the Germans to have turned the Channel Isles into one huge Concentration Camp without the knowledge of the people on the mainland.

Slave labour, which was expendable, was used for building the tunnels and the fortifications. It has been disclosed that the extermination of the civil population of the Islands had been planned thus total secrecy would have been achieved. (See Margaret Brockley's testimony).

In the latter part of 1944 following D-Day when the German Forces and the Islanders were all starving Vice-

Admiral Friedrich Huffmeier expressed the opinion (in a message relayed to Hitler) that the Islands could hold out to the end of 1945 but the civilian population would have to be eliminated.

The question of whether or not the elimination of the civilian population would be necessary is also referred to in a portion of Baron Von Aufsess' diary. A comment softened by a note that this would be regrettable and he hoped such a course would not become necessary. (Baron Von Aufsess was chief of administration in the Kommandantur, a man of high German birth and friendly with a number of the Channel Islands Administration personnel). His statement was evidently made with some relief in the knowledge that such a decision would be made at a higher level than his own.

In the official history of the Occupation commissioned in 1970 by the States of Jersey and Guernsey and Alderney and the Chief Pleas of Sark and written by Dr Charles Cruickshank there is a remarkable absence of detail about the treatment of Jews and the legislation taken against them by the Germans. The information was available, thus leaving it open to speculation as to why such a wealth of detail should have been ignored.

As the book abounds with a wealth of information, in detail, about a number of aspects of little or no importance to the story of the Occupation it can only be assumed that the omissions were made under direction or a personal whim.

That an anti-semitic attitude had existed officially in the Channel Islands for centuries was no secret for the enviable titles of Bailiff, Law Officer and Jurat both in Jersey and Guernsey were closed to Roman Catholics, Jews and Freethinkers.

The bar was more rigorously applied in Guernsey than in Jersey.

It is not surprising therefore to find in the books about the Occupation – with the exception of one – a minimum of reference paid to the problems and fate of the Channel Island Jews.

The fact that the Jews were few in number seems to have been taken as sufficient reason by everyone concerned for ignoring the treatment to which they were subjected. Some were sent to Auschwitz and never returned.

Should numbers matter in these circumstances?

In this behaviour we see a reflection of the attitude of the German population to the anti-Jewish activities of the Nazi party before the war.

Hitler's belief that he would find little opposition to his occupying forces must have been strengthened when he received reports from a spy who had, before the war, lived for months on the Channel Islands. The reports must have provided the information that Jews were not permitted to take part in any form of Island administration.

Major Ambrose Sherwill in his unpublished memoirs regrets the fact that he did not do more to shield what Jews there were on the Island of Guernsey with the excuse that he thought there were 'hardly any'. There were no Jews on the Island because they had already been sent to Auschwitz.

Sherwill's failure to defend the Jews at that time might have encouraged the Todt Organisation Commandants to greater atrocities against the Jewish prisoners who later flooded into Alderney.

Major Sherwill must have been aware of the measures against the Jews, published in early 1940, by the Civil Commandant, they read as follows:-

1) Persons of Jewish religion, or who have more than two Jewish grandparents, are deemed to be Jews.

2) Jews who have fled from occupied Zones may not return there.

3) Every Jew must present himself for registration with his family.

4) Every business conducted by a Jew is to be designated a 'Jewish undertaking' in English, French & German.

5) Heads of Jewish communities must furnish all necessary documentary evidence.

6) Contravention is punishable by imprisonment, fine and confiscation of goods.

Some weeks later this order was supplemented by the following further demands.

1) A declaration of all shares belonging to or pledged to Jews.

2) A statement of their beneficial interest in any business.

3) A statement of their sleeping interest in any such business

4) Particulars of any real estates held, or interest therein.

5) All legal transactions by Jews whereby goods were disposed of after May 23rd 1940 were to be declared null and void.

6) An Administrator for Jewish undertakings was to be appointed.

A further edict appeared on 31st may 1941 stating that anyone having three grandparents of Jewish blood or two grandparents married to Jews were deemed to be Jews. A number of crippling constrictions were imposed also and to add to their misery a special curfew became operative on 26th June 1942 from 8 p.m. to 6 a.m.

If the Bailiff did not believe there were any Jews left in the Island then the Germans evidently did. Finally, all Jews were deported to Germany.

A student of the activities of the National Socialist Party in Germany against Jews would recognise in the foregoing details a replica of the manner in which the Jewish community was progressively and systematically disintegrated and finally disposed of.

These facts are surely sufficient to remove doubts in anyone's mind that the Jewish population of Great Britain was destined for the same fate as had befallen the countries which the Nazis had already overrun.

On the 1st July 1940 the Bailiff of the States of Jersey received a communication from the Commander of the German Air Forces in Normandy. It demanded peaceful surrender of the Island and required white flags and crosses to be displayed everywhere which had to remain in place until occupation by the German troops.

Reprisals were threatened for hostile acts, the cessation of communication with Britain was demanded and the Island Authorities were required to be in attendance at the Airport until occupation.

Clause 8 in the communication declared the following: ...

'In case of peaceful surrender, the lives, property and liberty of peaceful inhabitants are solemnly guaranteed'.

But what really happened?

The persecution of the Jews and final deportation began immediately, as has been described, next came the imprisonment of anyone, including women, who provoked them in the smallest way and then gradually the deportation of more than 2000 people to Concentration Camps in France and Germany who could not prove full birth rights as a true Islander.

They had committed no crime.

This then was the solemn guarantee to all peaceful inhabitants as it was interpreted by the German Nazis. Who then would have believed any promise or guarantee made by a German to a British Government had Britain capitulated?

With the experience of the solemn undertaking given to Chamberlain by Hitler in 1938 staring them in the face it seemed there were many people both in the Channel Islands and in Britain both amongst the population and in authority who still believed anything the Nazis promised.

In fact the Nazis, despite their suspicion that Britain, once conquered, would prove to be as cooperative as the Vichy Government, would have had no option, in pursuance of their adopted policies and the theories laid down in *Mein Kampf*, but to extend their programme of the 'Final Solution' to Britain and remove all the known Jews.

Along with these would have gone the known anti-Fascist notabilities ... 2820 of them ... all listed in the infamous 'Black Book' discovered in SS Archives at the cessation of war.

The Germans, both before and during the war, had learned that even amongst their most loyal and enthusiastic followers there was a limit to which atrocities could be exposed publicly.

Aware of the pro-German sympathies within the British Establishment the Germans would have wished to avoid upsetting those individuals, consequently the extermination programme would have been carried out as discreetly as possible and out of reach of prying eyes.

Hitler had no wish to unnecessarily antagonise world opinion. Approval of the Third Reich whilst achieving its objectives was paramount.

Hitler was only too well aware of the strong opposition President Roosevelt had encountered in the first years of the war from the American Nazi Party, the German element of the population and the 'this is not our war' lobby in the Senate. With a victory over Britain this would almost certainly have strengthened.

Hitler therefore, both in Britain, when conquered, and in America, had to keep a clean nose.

So ... ... for the execution of the British holocaust what better place than the Channel Islands?

Hitler had already issued strong directives that the Channel islands must be turned into an impregnable fortress. They did, in fact, become the most heavily defended coastlines in Europe.

Why ... if Hitler was confident of success, did he order that the two largest 'underground hospitals' in the world should be built in Jersey and Guernsey?

It is illogical to suppose that Hitler and his hierarchy or the German High Command could have believed they could have been of any use during or after the successful invasion of Britain.

The transportation of ill or injured soldiers to such inaccessible places would have been costly and inefficient and caused delays in dealing with the sick. Hospitals would almost certainly have already been established in France, or could have been, and would have provided all the necessary services with greater facility.

Hitler had, on one occasion, announced that the Channel Isles were to be the playground of the Master Race. Why build such huge unhealthy, unpleasant places for holidaymakers?

There is little doubt that the building of the 'underground hospitals' had some purpose other than that publicly stated.

The Germans had already made a model of the large Verelat tunnel complex on the south east coast of Jersey. In Jersey there were 26 tunnels and more unfinished, whilst in Guernsey there were 41 tunnels. Many of the entrances have now been blocked up and have become covered in undergrowth.

It is surely reasonable to ask for what purpose were the Germans building mile upon mile of tunnel?

Sidney Bernstein's film of German concentration and experimentation Camps was intended to be an official record, a montage, of films taken by British, American and Russian Government Agencies. It was intended to be a permanent proof to those who did not believe such things had happened.

Originally commissioned by the British Government (amongst whom were some of the greatest sceptics) through the Supreme Command of the Psychological Warfare Division and created with the assistance of a team of top journalists and advisers and edited by Mr. Alfred Hitchcock, it was first encouraged and then discouraged on the grounds – so the reason was first given – that it was too horrific, too shocking, for general release. So it was banned much to the chagrin and disappointment of Sidney Bernstein and all those who had contributed to its making and suffered from having to be 'there'.

It has been released only twice, in 1985 by Granada Television and again on the death of Sidney Bernstein, on February 5th 1944 as a tribute to one of his greatest achievements.

Why was the film banned? Had Sidney Bernstein done too good a job and created an embarrassing situation for the British Government? And surely, not out of consideration for the tender and sensitive feelings of the British public but out of consideration for the Germans!

Lord Annan of Political Division, Control Commission Germany – at the end of the film, offers the specious argument that it was much more important to help the Germans restore their country and economy than to spend time proving that the whole nation had taken part in a journey back 12 thousand years into total barbarism.

In a Berlin which was a heap of rubble at the end of the war people were dying from disease and starvation at 4000 per day. This figure, quite coincidentally, happened to be the same figure set by the Nazis as a desirable target for their extermination camps once fitted with the new and improved design gaschambers and incinerators referred to later in this book.

Perhaps Lord Annan was unaware of this, and, even if he had been, would it have made any difference to the official British line on how to conduct affairs now the war was over?

At Auschwitz, following earlier improvements in the disposal techniques 450,000 were incorrectly said to have been exterminated in three months, the same number of Jews as were living in Britain at that time.

In Bernstein's film there is pictorial evidence supported by narration that a 'hospital' had been built close to a complex of underground tunnels being used as a rocket factory.

It is interesting to note that the measurements of many of the galleries and tunnels were similar to those in the 'underground hospitals' in Jersey and Guernsey.

The rocket factory was the notorious V1/V2 complex which came to be known as 'Dora' and was dug deep into Mount Kohnstein following the destruction of Peenemunde by Allied bombing.

Although not classified as a 'concentration' camp conditions and treatment of prisoners were worse than many concentration camps.

As is Alderney, the striped pyjamas typical of the concentration camps were worn by all prisoners working there, and the terrible place was the scene of more deaths than many of the official concentration camps.

In less than two years it is known that more than 20,000 prisoners died. Unrecorded deaths were estimated at double that number out of the 60,000 alleged to have worked there.

The 'hospital' which was nothing more than a shed, was built close to the incinerators and before the arrival of the liberating Americans the death rate of prisoners in the camp had reached such proportions the incinerators were unable to cope.

As the 3rd Armoured Division of the 1st United States Army approached some of the remaining prisoners were marched away by the Nazis, 4000 were too ill to be moved and by the time the Americans arrived to the scene of horror only 450 were found alive.

The dead had been stacked in piles, some of the dead being stacked upon those still alive and about to die.

From 1933 euphemisms, such as 'work camp', 'rehousing' and 'rehabilitation' had been used to quieten the fears of those being transported. Whilst the addition of 'underground hospital' would have been nothing new there is no evidence the Germans ever referred to the tunnels in the Channel Islands by that name. It is likely that this title was applied by the Channel Islanders themselves because in the last few months of the war the occupying Germans used them for the wounded and ill troops escaping from the Allied troops of the Normandy invasion.

Later it was a convenient 'label' and less horrific for the tourists who were later to become regular visitors to the tunnels. Whilst referring to 'euphemisms' it is well to remember the words above the gateway to Auschwitz ... **'Arbeit Macht Frei' ... 'Work Frees You'**. In other words, this is where you are worked to death!

On May 9th 1994 BBC 2 Horizon programme showed a film titled 'The Blue Prints of Genocide'. The film provided evidence that the development of the gas-chambers and the crematoriums had been on a haphazard basis. Greater efficiency was required so Architects, Engineers, Builders and Oven manufacturers were recruited to design the ultimate in the machinery of mass extermination.

These methods were being reflected in the building operations in the Channel Islands.

Let us not blind ourselves to the fact that one of the main planks of the Nazi cult was the belief the Germans were a master race. The 'purification' of the German Race and, in fact, of the whole of Europe meant the total extinction of the Jewish race at all levels of Society. Also included were Gipsies, Slavs and many more.

Within the Third Reich hierarchy Hitler had selected for the direction of sociological, psychological and racial policy the most intelligent of them all, Dr Joseph Paul Goebbels.

He had graduated in philosophy at Heidelberg in 1921.

In a speech in 1933 he made the following statement ...

"We want no more stupid, absurd statements to the effect that the Jew is a human being"

Hitler had become convinced that Freemasonry had become the tool of the Jews and was, therefore, intent upon wiping out the Freemasons also, if declaration of their membership was not disclosed.

An extension of the 'Final Solution' programme seemed likely beyond the elimination of the Jewish race hence the need to perfect the machinery for that purpose. (See Chapter 'Gaschambers')

For example the infamous *'Black Book'* lists the United Grand Lodge of the English Freemasons for immediate occupation and interrogation of the members.

Is it therefore remarkable, that some of the Guernsey authorities might have felt a degree of sympathy and agreement with the German ideals and purposes? We do not know of course, who, if anyone, in the Guernsey hierarchy had read *'Mein Kampf'*. To have done so is to become aware of the eventual purpose of Hitler and his National Socialist Party.

There were many in the British Establishment and Government who should have done so, but had not read *'Mein Kampf'*, and these included the King, Mr. Chamberlain and Lord Halifax. Quizzical as it may seem nor had Hitler's greatest friend Albert Speer, according to his own testimony.

But there was one **very** influential lady who, it is alleged, **had** read it ... the Queen herself (now the Queen Mother) and it is said, she took it upon herself to send a copy in November 1939 (a little late in the day perhaps) to Lord Halifax with the following admonition ...

"I advise you not to read it ... or you might go mad and that would be a great pity. Even a skip through gives one a good idea of his mentality, ignorance and obvious sincerity". (Did she mean 'insincerity'?)

Halifax, like Chamberlain and the King, was a confirmed appeaser and would probably not have appreciated the sentiments expressed in *'Mein Kampf'*. Were either of these three Freemasons? We shall never know for such things are secret. We **do** know however that both Halifax and Chamberlain, together with Churchill and Beaverbrook are all listed in *'The Black Book'* for arrest and presumably imprisonment and eventual extermination, probably on the grounds of being 'war criminals' or perhaps Freemasons?

The King had more than once come close to overstepping his constitutional 'boundaries', no less so than in his dealings with Halifax and Chamberlain but it would seem he had almost reached the unacceptable in his involvement with the move to destabilise and finally remove the war Secretary Mr. Hore-Belisha.

Mr. Hore-Belisha was a Jew.

Rumours were that this was the reason.

Why did the King want him removed?

Was it because he too was anti-semitic ... or at least taking the advice of those who were?

Perhaps it is worthy of a pause here to remember it was not until 26th July 1858 ... eighty one years to the outbreak of World War Two ... that Jews were permitted to take a seat in Parliament.

It was Sir Robert Inglis, Tory member for Oxford, who in the 1840s during a speech in Parliament said ...

"Two centuries ago there was not one single Jew in this realm of England ... they came in drop by drop, preserving their own inherent and insoluble character. Did we invite them? – did they come in for our convenience? – did they not come in for their own? ... can they ever, as true Jew, be amalgamated with us? ..."

Note: Not many years later a Jew became one of the finest Prime Ministers this country has had.

Whatever may be, The Secretary of State for War, Mr. Hore-Belisha, the ambitious, energetic Jew with a hatred of the Germans as fierce as that of Winston Churchill burning within him, was being as successful in his efforts on behalf of the Army as Lord Beaverbrook was for the Air Force.

The strength of antagonism towards Hore-Belisha was so great even Winston Churchill, who supported him, failed to prevent his removal. He was manoeuvred from his office amid a chorus of protestations that 'it was not because he was a Jew'.

If he was being successful at his job, for what reason, then, was he being sacked? It does seem that more attention was being paid to 'personalities' than to the paramount need to win the war!

From the moment he became Prime Minister Churchill was fighting an uphill battle contending with internecine fighting which should have ceased once war was declared.

This frequent involvement with personalities and their protection... 'personal sensitivities' is the official terminology... runs like a trip-wire through much of the investigations covered by this book and the efforts of others with a similar objective.

There seems little doubt that some of the delays experienced by the Bailiffs of Jersey and Guernsey in obtaining replies to urgent matters was due to the departmental infighting going on in Whitehall.

It seems unlikely, even if Hitler's sources of Intelligence had dwindled on the outbreak of war, that he was not fully aware of the conflicting opinions and feelings being expressed within the British establishment.

Hitler was also no doubt aware of the King's strong German ancestry, remembering that his father King George V was forced to change his family name of Saxe-Coburg-Gotha to Windsor during the First World War because of strong anti-german public opinion. Hitler must also have been aware that King George V had also, under the Royal Guelphic Order, retained the more ancient German lineage name of Guelph.

The names appearing in 'The Black Book' – of which more later, bear the evidence required that before the outbreak of war a considerable degree of meticulous research had been conducted. The German Administration knew exactly from whom to expect opposition and from whom to expect support and information once they had achieved victory.

In 'The Black Book' Mr. Hore-Belisha is listed for 'arrest' and his sacking would not have gone unnoticed or remarked in Germany. It would have provided further fuel for their belief that there was in Great Britain a strong anti-semitic feeling in the upper echelons of society and within the Army.

AND WHAT, IT MAY BE ASKED, HAS ALL THIS TO DO WITH NAZI ATROCITIES IN ALDERNEY AND GAS CHAMBERS IN THE CHANNEL ISLES?

It is very simple. The Channel Islands would be the prototype for the occupation of Britain.

The treatment of the Jews in Jersey and Guernsey demonstrated the meticulous efficiency with which the Germans dealt with each problem, large or small, and their complete, unswerving, adherence to their established patterns of behaviour.

Hitler, if his policy of 'Final Solution' must succeed must apply it to Great Britain. If the execution of that policy was too obvious he would almost certainly meet objections from the British pro-Fascist, anti-semitic lobby. So what better place than the Channel Islands well removed from observations?

The circumstantial evidence of such a plan is there to see.

In 'Mein Kampf', page after page is devoted to a study of the Jew in world society, almost 50 pages in all, dealing with every aspect of life and their achievements.

In 'Mein Kampf', Hitler is committed to the extermination of all Jews. One aspect of his philosophies which is not covered is the means of disposal, but by 1945 this problem was being dealt with with typical Teutonic thoroughness and efficiency.

In 1945 when Allied Troops, British, American and Russian arrived at the various camps spread throughout occupied Europe they found that the death rate in Mauthausen, for example, had reached 300 per day from gassings, starvation and disease and Dachau and Buchenwald had accounted for 820,000.

In the various extermination camps in Poland the figures were .....

Chelmno	152,000
Belzec	600,000
Sobibor	250,000
Auschwitz – Birkenhau	1,000,000
Treblinka	900,000
Majdanek	80,000

but these figures, totalling 2,982,000 represent only the tip of the iceberg, and represent only Jews. The total number of Jews murdered by the Nazis is generally believed to be in the region of 6,000,000, but even this appalling figure pales into insignificance when those who died in work camps, concentration and detention camps from overwork, starvation, beatings and disease are considered. The figure is disputed but is rarely less than 10,000,000. We shall never know.

In April 1945 it was believed that the Todt Organisation was using the following workforce spread throughout Europe ...

Deutsches Reich:	165,000	Albanian:	591
Österreich:	65,459	Griechenland:	59,185
Luxembourg:	1200	Bulgarien:	11,393
Frankreich:	76,134	Jugoslawlen:	65,000
Belgien:	32,000	Ungarm:	550,000
Niederlande:	102,000	Teschechoslowakel:	143,000
Danemark:	116	Rumánien:	211,214
Norwegen:	758	Polen:	2,700,000
Italien:	6513	Sowjetunion:	2,100,000

Any suggestion that any othr fate awaited the 450,000 Jews in Britain during the war, other than complete extinction, is fallacious, and in open contradiction to the evidence.

The figure of 450,000 is based on Synagogue membership returns and estimates from refugee organisations supplied by The Board of Deputies of British Jews.

At the time however, considerable numbers of refugees were flooding into Britain and had done so since 1931 when the first signs of what was about to happen in Germany became evident.

Listed below are 42 of the many talented men and women who arrived in Britain and found recognition in the fields of Law, Science, Medicine, Philosophy, Banking, Publishing and The Arts.

Of these 20 are still living and 11 are listed in 'The Black Book'.

The Law
* Ernst Joseph Cohn
* David Daube
* Sir Otto Kahn-Fruend
Rt. Hon. Sir Michael Kerr
Frederick Honig

Science, Medicine and Philosophy
Charlotte Auerbach
Sir Herman Bondi
Hans Bethe
* Sir Ernst Boris Chain
Sigmund Freud
* Herbert Frohlich
Sir Ludwig Guttman
Dennis Gabor
Bernhard Katz
Sir Hans Adolf Krebs
Sir Rudolf Peierls
Sir Karl Popper

Banking
Friedrich Von Hayek
Lord Roll
* Sir Siegmund George Warburg

Publishing
Andre Deutsch
Paul Hamyln
Walter Neurath
Lord Weidenfeld

The Arts
* Frank Auerbach
Elizabeth Bergner
Norbert Brainin
* Lucian Freud
Sir Ernst Gombrich
Eric Hobsbawm
Arthur Koestler
* Sir Alexander Korda
* Sir Claus Moser
Siegmund Nissel
* Sir Nikolaus Pevsner
Emeric Pressburger
Peter Schidlof
Sir Sigmund Sternberg
Victor Weisz (Vicky)

Politics
Thomas Balogh
Nikki Kaldor

Business
Lord Peter Bauer

Those with this asterisk * are listed in 'The Black Book'

As it was the policy of the Nazis to eliminate all intellectuals not of pure Aryan blood it may be assumed that eventually every name on this list would have been sought out by the Gestapo.

Would the Germans, once British capitulation had been achieved, have allowed any significant degree of autonomy to the pro-Fascist thinkers in the government? It is extremely unlikely.

Hitler and the German hierarchy, before the war, had made some overtures to the British. In fact within *'Mein Kampf'* the suggestion is made that following a peaceful capitulation, the British could be left to run the Empire whilst Hitler and his Nazis ran Europe and the Near East. Communism would have been defeated. There would have been no threat to Britain from that direction and America, too, would have breathed a sigh of relief.

To many in the British ruling classes this could have been a tempting prospect. The crippling expense of a long drawn out war would have been avoided and life for most would have proceeded, so they believed, much as it had always done.

With the fear of Communism running high, as it was in the 1930s, what better prospect than to let someone else ... Hitler and his Nazis ... deal with the Communists?

Was this the essence of the message which Hess, when he landed in Scotland on 10th may 1941, wished to convey? He had hoped to visit the Duke of Hamilton who was a known pro-Fascist. However, all that may be, he failed! And five days later Hitler invaded the USSR.

Had Chamberlain still been Prime Minister it is open to speculation as to whether the visit would have been treated more seriously.

Fortunately for the British and unfortunately for Hitler, Winston Churchill was Prime Minister and determined to win the war and free Europe and the world.

Temporary appeasement had preceded almost every German acquisition, if this was the purpose of Hess' visit, as has been suggested, would future events have followed a similar pattern? Perhaps with Chamberlain but not with Winston Churchill.

The extent of the difficulties with which Winston Churchill had to contend in the Government and the Establishment are almost beyond the commonsense belief of the ordinary man.

Lord Beaverbrook, loyalist, fanatically pro-Empire, proprietor of the highly successful and influential 'Daily Express' and who proved to be an outstanding figure in the war effort by his success with the Aircraft Industry was Winston Churchill's choice for the job, but his choice was made against the wishes of the King and Queen.

The Palace had not wanted Lord Beaverbrook in a position of importance any more than they wanted Winston Churchill as Prime Minister who was finally and reluctantly appointed on 10th May 1940.

Hess arrived in Scotland on 10th May 1941!! Exactly one year too late!

Chamberlain, despite his pitiful performance in handling the war effort received support from the Palace right up to the last. Would he, one wonders, had he stayed, have lost us the war?

Speeches and comments of a damaging and derogatory nature about Winston Churchill made in and out of Parliament and by members of the House of Lords, would have earned the epithet of 'treason' and execution would have followed had they been made against Hitler by any of his hierarchy.

On one occasion Lord Salisbury, it is alleged, complained that expenditure on the war effort should be checked. He wanted 'war on the cheap', for it was, he said 'affecting the share prices', whilst Headlam's concern was not victory over the Germans but that 'such expenditure must mean higher taxes!' Well!!!

How Hitler must have chuckled and strutted when brought reports of the internecine goings on in the British Administration both civil and military.

Almost certainly, Hitler received reports on the apparent willingness of the Channel Islands States to assist, without protest, the German Occupation Forces from the earliest days.

A report from the Feldkommandant of Guernsey to Hitler described the Guernsey inhabitants as 'obsequious peasants'.

A comment no doubt intended to massage the Fuhrer's ego and bring the Feldkommandant to his Fuhrer's notice. But is it surprising that in the early days of the war Hitler believed Britain would either agree to collaborate or would prove an easy victory? And is it surprising that in such circumstances no official nomenclature was given by the Germans to the dozens of tunnels created in the Islands?

As has already been remarked the pressures upon the civil population of a small island such as Guernsey or Jersey must have been much greater than those experienced by the populations of the occupied nations.

In Guernsey and Jersey, for the many, there was no escape. For those who felt more strongly the desire to take sabotage action against the Germans the frustration must have been unbearable for had they done so reprisals on their families and the rest of the population would have swiftly followed, as evidenced by Joe Miere's story told in this book.

For example: On 28th September 1940 a brightly coloured poster announced in English and German that Marcel Brossier had been sentenced to death and had been shot for cutting a telephone cable.

A further announcement, a month or so later informed everyone that for releasing a carrier pigeon (presumably with a message for England) Louis Berrier had been sentenced to death and shot.

To emphasis their thoroughness and following an announcement that no pigeons could be kept by anyone, the edict was extended to **all** pigeons.

For over a century almost tame pigeons had habitually filled the pavement of Royal Square, St. Helier, Jersey and had been a delight to everyone. They were caught by the Germans, who with the same economical thoroughness with which they had preserved and collected gold teeth, hair, spectacles and other belongings of the gaschamber victims, ensured that the pigeons would form a welcome change of diet for the dinner table at the German Officer's Mess.

And so it went on, without so far as is known, any objection from the Island Authorities.

The Germans had once again demonstrated, as they had done in Germany, and again in Vichy France, that all kinds of atrocities could be conducted under the noses of the population without a word of protest.

The Jews were no more an embarrassment to the Island Authorities for they had long ago been sent to concentration camps in Europe.

The question then arises 'were the Channel Islands being used as an experiment, a testing ground, of the behaviour of British subjects under Nazi domination?' Would the British have collaborated, gone along with the extermination of the Jews, following defeat or capitulation?

Had many of the Channel Islanders when watching the plight of the Jews in their midst before deportation said to themselves 'there but for the grace of **another** God go I'?

'Behave yourselves, do as you are told, do not oppose us in any way and you will not be hurt' was the message which was being conveyed to the population over and over again.

On 17th March a poster appeared stating that François Marie Scornet had been executed by shooting.

Scornet was a young Frenchman who had landed by accident in Jersey with a group of boys who had escaped from France. Scornet was accused of 'favouring the actions of the enemy by wilfully supporting England in the war against the German Empire!'.

The Rev. Pere Maré, a Catholic Priest, gave Scornet his last rites whilst he was already pinioned to an oak tree. His last words were 'Long Live God! Long Live France!'

Of Scornett's fifteen companions four died in captivity.

The populations of the Islands, faced with demonstrations of such ruthlessness and the difficulties on such small islands of conducting any useful and effective guerilla reprisals, without endangering the entire community, appeared to be acquiescent, and have been accused of cooperation.

Would the British have behaved any differently?

The testimonies of the contributors to this book confirm the difficulties of living under such conditions and in such circumstances.

The fate of the Jews in Britain would have been the same as those in the Channel Islands and the millions already murdered throughout Europe.

English nationals and Jews had already been dealt with and deported and were in prison camps or had been killed.

It has been claimed that the Bailiffs of both Jersey and Guernsey knew nothing of what was going on in Alderney. Whilst this might be true of Jersey it is difficult to accept for Guernsey.

The Guernsey States Authorities had, throughout the occupation, done everything possible to please and appease the German Civil and Military Authorities but they were to find that, as the years passed, the German attitude would steadily harden.

Almost from the beginning the Germans had demanded that Guernsey workers should be sent to Alderney. Guernsey had suggested that a small number of workers, largely artisans, could do useful work repairing damaged and vandalised houses. Once there however the Military treated them as prisoners of war and required attendance on morning parades and imposed a curfew.

Food was bad and their living conditions very poor. They were not permitted to leave and became virtual prisoners their treatment being a total violation of International Law.

Later, when many more troops had arrived in Alderney and the prison camps were being built demands were made to the States Authorities by the Nazi Administration for more workers.

Guernsey acceded to this demand by instructing the States Labour Office to issue dismissal notices to over 1000 of the greenhouse industry workers. With the dismissal notice went an advice that employment could be found by applying to the German Administration and to the Todt Organisation.

Some of the workers, after a spell working in Alderney under conditions to those similar to the first batch of 30, reported what they had seen of the horrors there.

Against the Hague Convention and all International laws of war some had been made to work on Military Installations.

Their protests were ignored.

So much for peaceful cooperation!

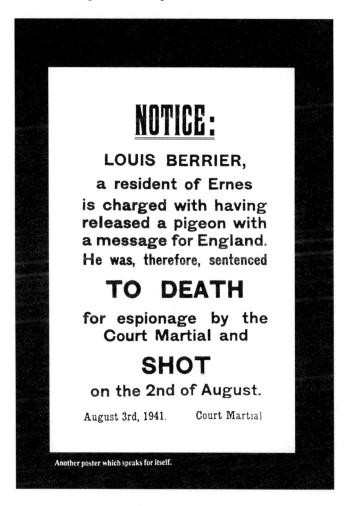

NOTICE:

LOUIS BERRIER,

a resident of Ernes

is charged with having released a pigeon with a message for England. He was, therefore, sentenced

TO DEATH

for espionage by the Court Martial and

SHOT

on the 2nd of August.

August 3rd, 1941.   Court Martial

Another poster which speaks for itself.

NOTICE.

ORDER OF THE FIELD COMMANDANT.

On or before the 5th day of November, 1940, every person who is sheltering a person of any of the following classes must make the report hereinafter ordered :

1. British subjects not of Jersey birth, with the exception of those who had their permanent residence in the Island before the 1st September, 1939.

2. British subjects who have come to the Island since the German occupation.

3. British subjects, including natives of the Island, who had left the Island before the German occupation and who have returned since.

Whoever, after the 5th day of November, 1940, continues to shelter a British subject of any of the foregoing classes without having made the required report, or who subsequently shelters or conceals a British subject of any of the foregoing classes, particularly members of the British Armed Forces, shall be shot.

Reports are to be made in writing to the Attorney-General, States Offices, St. Helier, not later than 5 p.m. on Tuesday, November 5th, 1940.

The Field Commander,

SCHUMACHER,

November 1st, 1940.   Colonel.

WHY GO MAD?

**COMPULSORY
EVACUATION**

A LIE!

There's No PLace
LIKE HOME

CHEER UP!

The poster by Bailiff Coutanche, before the arrival of the Germans, persuading Jersey Islanders not to leave.

Was he right?

GUILTY MEN

Four camps were set up in Alderney. Three ... Borkum, Nordeney and Helgoland were run by the infamous Todt Organisation. These camps held men prisoners of all nationalities. Their purpose was to provide slave labour for the army. German Todt workers were confined to Borkum whilst other nationalities, a high proportion of them from the Soviet Union, occupied Nordeney and Helgoland.

All the prisoners were made to wear stripped pyjamas as a uniform and had cropped heads and numbered identification.

The most feared camp of all, run on concentration camp lines, was Sylt under the direct control of the SS. Head of this camp, the only concentration camp on British soil, was Commandant SS Sturmbahnfuhrer Maximilian List. Under his command the prisoners were subjected to the most appalling treatment and torture on a daily basis.

List was not the only Nazi guilty of atrocities. In charge of the Nordeney camp was Karl Theiss alleged to be equally guilty of brutality and torture of the prisoners in the camp.

Finally there was Kurt Klebeck. Kurt Klebeck was in Alderney during the earlier years of the occupation and is alleged to have been guilty of torture, brutality and other forms of atrocities whilst in command.

Evidence of this was required and it was believed to lie in the 33 files held in the Guernsey archives since 1945 and not for release until 2045.

Labour MP Mr. David Winnick made his first approach to the Attorney General (Rt. Hon. Sir Nicholas Lyell QC) through a Parliamentary Question for a priority written answer. (See Document No. 3) How many years Klebeck served of his 10-year sentence for his crimes in Russia is not known. It is believed he now lives in Hamburg.

The extent of David Winnick's efforts, his difficulties in bringing to justice the Alderney Nazi war criminals and in obtaining the release of the secret Guernsey files can only be appreciated by a study of the letters exchanged with the various Government Departments and the German Embassy.

It will be seen that in Document No. 4 the German Ambassador Baron Hermann von Richthofen is hiding behind the fact that no 'incriminating material has been made available to them'.

The incriminating material was of course still under wraps in the Guernsey Archives.

In Document No. 6 (a letter to Prime Minister John Major) the article referred to by Mr. Winnick in the *'Mail on Sunday'* appeared on August 2nd 1992. The *'Mail on Sunday'* claimed the documents had come into their possession and the evidence was there to be seen.

The Prime Minister's reply on 7th August is interesting if nothing!

On 14th August *'The Guardian'* took up the battle quoting from documents to be found in the Public Record Office in which investigations by the Civil Affairs Unit made in May 1945 revealed that "a number of people acted in an unseemly, undesirable or even disgraceful way" during the occupation.

Twelve cases were passed on to the Director of Public Prosecutions, who, whilst agreeing there was a prima facie case, did nothing.

Apparently, in 1943, 'collaboration' which was a crime under the Defence of the Realm Act, was repealed in the Channel Islands.

It is at this point that the smell of 'cover up' becomes so strong it cannot be ignored. The question is again raised 'Why?'

In 1943 there had been a landing of a British 'spy' on Guernsey. It was successful and the invader had returned to England with 'information which might be of assistance in determining the German garrison's organisation, strength and defences which might oppose any British landing attempt'.

The reports back to England, so The Viscount Cranbourne's letter (Document No. 18) from the Ministry of Defence claims, 'were not part of the War Office's post-liberation war crimes investigations'. Again ... 'Why?'

The information which they, the raiders, had obtained on German defences could be of no possible importance 49 years later, so what else was in those reports?

Was the report of collaboration so shocking, so shaming, that in order to absolve the Authorities from possible future trial the Defence of the Realm Act was immediately repealed for Guernsey?

Information regarding the atrocities on Alderney was not available in the 26 files released to the Public Records office in December 1992. Viscount Cranbourne's letter is dated 17th February 1993!

What else, in addition to military intelligence, was contained in those reports? Was it that because of the very high degree of collaboration all the files were shelved for 100 years? Or was it simply a 'device' that such action should be taken by the British Government in order to save the face of the Guernsey authorities? If not, why the careful phrasing of the Press Release (Document No. 13) announcing that 'The Home office will announce on 30th November (1992) that the review of Home Office papers relating to the wartime Nazi occupation of the Channel Islands is complete. The result is that the Home Office is holding 7 files on extended closure under section 5 (1) of the Public Record Act 1958.

The vast majority of files will be opened to public inspection however, including 16 files where information has been extracted from certain documents because of 'personal sensitivity', or in two instances on the grounds of 'national security'.

Is it then because of **'personal sensitivity'** that the remaining 7 files are being held?

Another interesting revelation is found in Document No. 21, a letter from Mr. Michael Jack, of the Home Office to Mr.

David Winnick. The significant words are these ... "A recent development is that the Home Office has now received a request from the German Judicial Authorities for the production of information relating to allegations of crimes committed on the Channel Islands during World War II by **persons working for the occupying German authorities"**. Presumably none other than the Todt Organisation? Or were they hinting that Guernseymen may be implicated?

Who is being shielded? Is this to be interpreted as a threat or a hint to 'lay off' by the Germans?

In addition to Kurt Klebeck, SS Col. Maximilian List and Karl Theiss there are a further ten all of whom are still alive and free and two of whom, at least, are still in this country and having adopted British nationality are allegedly indictable.

These are:

Siemion Serafimowicz,
Anton Grecas,
Andre Bakunowicz,
Alexander Schewidler,
Stasic Chren Owski (alias Stanislaw Chrzanowski)
Wilhelm Mohnke,
Arthur Rudolph of Dora,
Paul Touvier,
Erich Priebke.

Then there is:

Professor Dr Franz Six, better known as SS Colonel Professor Dr. Frank Six who was to have headed the SS operations in Britain.

Six was already notorious and responsible for wholesale massacres in the Soviet Union. He was sentenced in 1948 at Nuremberg as a war criminal to 20 years in prison but was released 4 years later by the Americans and the British to act as a spy in Soviet Russia in company with a number of his SS and Gestapo colleagues.

But despite all the efforts of Mr. David Winnick MP by asking question of the Prime Minister and writing to the Attorney General; the German Ambassador; William

Waldergrave MP then Minister of Public Service and Sciences; the then Secretary of State at the Home Office, the Rt. Hon. Kenneth Clarke QC MP; the then Rt. Hon. Malcolm Rifkind QC MP, Secretary of State at The Ministry of Defence and The Viscount Cranborne at the Ministry of Defence, Mr. David Winnick failed to obtain a satisfactory reply.

As stated elsewhere a German law forbade the deportation or extradition of a German subject on German soil, guilty of a crime on foreign soil for trial outside Germany.

The reluctance of the German Authorities, even as long as 22 years later, to bring to justice known Nazis guilty of war time atrocities and living in Germany is understandable if not acceptable and no doubt accounts for the sluggishness in dealing with the matter.

So far not one of the three men accused of atrocities in Alderney during the occupation has been brought to trial. At least one of these men remained in Alderney **after** the war ceased, yet they were never apprehended.

The reluctance of the German Authorities to take action is almost matched by the British, who despite demands from all directions have continued to permit alleged known war time criminals to live in this country until very recently, without making any attempt to bring them to justice.

The fact that they are now old men should make no difference, When interviewed they appeared to show no concern or remorse for their actions. Other murderers have, after many years, been apprehended, tried and convicted and sent to prison, why not these?

On November 27th 1944 a small newspaper report appeared in the 'Sunday Express' stating that following an extensive and long drawn out investigation Scotland Yard had collated sufficient evidence to bring to trial two pensioners who will be accused of war crimes in which they were alleged to have ordered the mass execution of Jews during World War Two.

In charge of this massive operation will be Mr. John Nutting the Old Bailey's senior treasury counsel. The men concerned it is said are not Germans but Lithuanians or Latvians. The author believes that two of the men are amongst those listed on page {...} of this book.

Some indications of the seriousness of this latest move is provided by an allocation of £1 million to pay the Court costs.

The Attorney General Sir Nicholas Lyell QC, with whom lies the final decision, as the Government's senior law officer, will be under considerable pressure, for since the day war ceased there has been a strong lobby amongst MPs and the Establishment against war crime trials.

This no doubt accounts for the reluctance on the part of Whitehall and the war Office to expedite any actions which might progress efforts to bring war criminals to justice, **especially those involved in the Alderney atrocities.**

But is the climate of opinion in favour of war crimes trials swinging in favour of those who consider they should go ahead?

A purpose built bomb/bullet proof Court House has been built in the Hague in which it is planned to hold the first Bosnian was crimes trials. It is believed that the building is intended as a permanent International facility for the conduct of war crimes trials from any theatre of war throughout the world.

Is there any connection between this new facility in the Hague Court for conducting war crimes trails on neutral international territory and the recent flurry of activity in bringing to trial the alleged war criminals still free in this country?

The suggestion that only now have Scotland Yard found sufficient evidence to bring action is nonsense. The evidence has been available for years but has been ignored It was Mrs. Thatcher in 1991 who pressed for action to be taken.

Will the faces or the consciences of the anti-war crimes lobby be saved if the trials are held in the Hague and not in England?

And more interesting still, will the Germans now be persuaded that despite their anti-deportation and extradition laws protecting German war criminals they must release them for trial on International territory like every other nation?

That this will be resisted by the Germans there is no doubt. Due to an all too familiar bungle between the Foreign Office and our Diplomats a high ranking officer of the British Army found himself attending a wreath laying ceremony in Celle in honour of the Nazi SS dead. (See illustration of wanted Nazi war criminals). Prominent at the ceremony were dozens of ex SS officers all wearing ties which were strangely like twisted Swastika. All belonged to the organisation OdR Ritterkreuz. A powerful group which would undoubtedly fight hard to protect their colleagues.

Was Mohnke amongst those who attended the ceremony?

The British Government's official line, maintained since 1945, has been that almost all victims of the atrocities committed in Alderney were Spanish or Russian, (this in fact is not true), it was therefore, for the Soviet Union to bring prosecutions. But without help from the British Government, which they did not get, the Soviet Union could no nothing.

Certainly since the collapse of the Soviet Union the degree of communication and cooperation between the Soviet Union and other countries, including Britain, has improved.

One theory offered for the reluctance to bring Klebeck, List and Theiss to justice is that they might, in giving evidence, relate unpleasant stories regarding the degree of cooperation, and perhaps atrocities committed by Guernseymen and the Guernsey States Authorities.

Some credence attaches to this theory when taken into consideration with another, apparently unconnected matter ... the reason offered for the retention of the seven files in the letter to Mr. David Winnick MP from The Viscount Cranbourne at the Ministry of Defence. The letter states ... 'the files' ... 'cover the debriefing of the Military and Civil Intelligence organisations **during** rather than at the end of the war, of personnel who had information on the Channel Islands. Such people 'they had landed in Guernsey, obtained information and escaped back to England' were debriefed with the **primary** intention of obtaining the maximum amount of intelligence data relevant ... to a British landing attempt'.

The emphasis on 'primary' is the author's.

What else did these people discover? What stories did they have to tell of cooperation with the Germans? Did they obtain information on conditions in Alderney? If they did why did the Military wait till the end of the war before liberating the Islands?

Did these raiders return with information of greater importance than that which they had been sent to obtain? (See the exchange of letters between The Viscount Cranbourne and David Winnick).

Of one thing we **are** sure Winston Churchill was deeply involved in delaying the liberation of the Islands until eleven months beyond D-Day.

Was he sickened with the news brought back from Guernsey? Or was no attempt made to liberate the Islands militarily soon after D-Day for fear of causing heavy civilian casualties?

It would seem that no book yet written about this aspect of the Occupation and Liberation has found a satisfactory answer. Is it all part of the 'cover-up' and the reason for retaining the secret files?

That there **was** a 'cover-up' there is no doubt, that there was a degree of omission in Charles Cruickshank's book there is no doubt, some of which might have been due to information not then being available, fallibility or deliberate. Whilst mentioning Major Pantcheff's activities in investigating the Islands in 1945, he fails to mention a much more important report prepared by Major Sidney Cotton, Captain G.C. Kent and Major F.F. Haddock who visited Alderney camps in June 1945. (See Cruickshank's book pages 200-205).

Peter King in his book 'The Channel Islands War', published in 1991 had the advantage of information disclosed in the intervening 20 years, but even he (pages 131 to 140) failed to find any clue as to the extraordinary discrepancies in the numbers of deaths reported on the Islands, and finds himself with no alternative but to state 'Their report had vanished'.

This in fact is not true, but no blame to Peter King, for the Author whilst researching for information for this book in the Imperial War Museum Library stumbled upon a file of correspondence between Major Haddock and Brigadier R. Shapcott relating to this subject.

Under Ref: Misc 172 (Item 2640) there is an item of correspondence dated 21st May 1945 from Major F.F. Haddock TD (Major, Legal Staff Force 135 BLA to Brigadier H. Shapcott CBE MC at the Office of the Judge Advocate General).

Major Haddock reports that in 1942 the health situation on the Islands was so bad that a German Medical Commission was despatched to the Islands. (**Note:** Surely an indication that deaths were exceeding any reasonable expectation in the circumstances and that some solution must be found?)

Major Haddock's report then goes on to refer to rumours about graves containing as many as 15 to 20 bodies **although only marked as containing one**. Only 250 graves were recorded.

Major Haddock, it would seem, carried out a good deal of in-depth investigation including recording many personal interviews with witnesses in whom, it would seem, he had some confidence. These witnesses told stories of mass killings, many deaths and the disposal of bodies without records.

Major Haddock suggests that he should be permitted to take his investigations further in his note to Brigadier Shapcott. The reply he received was a curt note, without explanation, that he 'need take the enquiries no further'.

It was unfortunate for Major Haddock that he was ranked below Major Cotton in the line of command and it emerges in the correspondence between Major Haddock and Brigadier

Shapcott that there was a degree of friction (for whatever reason) between himself and Major Cotton.

Major Cotton it will be remembered had been content to accept the documentation on deaths left behind by the SS and the Todt Organisation as accurate. Was Major Cotton lazy, incompetent, naive or acting under orders?

A study of Major Haddock's reports and letters to Brigadier Shapcott (most of the letters were not relevant to the purpose of this book) did however indicate that from the outset, the Military Investigators were under pressure from the media for information.

As it is well known that the Military have always disliked and tried to avoid the media this may provide the answer to why investigations were terminated in what some people referred to as 'indecent haste' and consequently the inaccuracies.

Despite all this Major Haddock made three requests to Brigadier Shapcott for an assistant to help him with what had become a heavy workload but in response received a firm 'negative'.

Was it that the Judge Advocate's Office did not wish to become bogged down in a mass of paper work or was this all part of the 'Grand Plan' to 'sweep everything under the carpet'?

It is perhaps appropriate to record here that no effort has been made to confirm or disprove the rumours about graves containing as many as 15 or 20 bodies by the simple expedient of digging them up! It has never been done, and some of the places where a single body was marked as having been buried have vanished altogether.

When Major Cotton arrived in Guernsey in May 1945 he was commanding a team of officers from M19 (Haddock being one) and an Army legal adviser.

Their reports, kept under wraps until 1992 were cold, factual and dealt only with what was found.

Faced with the wholesale destruction of the camps which had been carried out by the camp Commandants and the Todt Organisation following D-Day and before they escaped Major Cotton's team had only the information and documentation which they had left behind, on which to base his reports. That information was of course false. It was the same problem which Allied investigators had met throughout Europe wherever they attempted to piece together a picture of what had actually happened. The official records of the dead prepared in meticulous fashion by the SS had to be used because there was nothing else except the testimonies of witnesses and rumour.

In 1943 in Alderney there were 3000 German troops and 5000 prisoners, to suggest therefore, that only 530 persons died during the Occupation of that Island is ludicrous.

As stated earlier Kurt Klebeck was allegedly responsible for 350 deaths. Are we expected to believe only 180 persons died from other causes? The reader does not need to be a pyrrhonist to treat such figures with contempt. Prisoners were starved, when they became too ill and too weak to work they were transferred to Neuengamme, the 'death' concentration camp close to Hamburg, to die.

Sylt, the SS concentration camp in Alderney, was responsible to the Command running Neuengamme. List and Theiss, it will be remembered had once been subject to disciplinary action because of their inefficiency in despatching a train load of dying prisoners to Neuengamme from Alderney. Certainly, if large numbers of those no longer capable of work were returned to Neuengamme this might be the explanation for the discrepancy in the figures.

It was never satisfactorily established whether the 350 souls murdered by Klebeck were included in the 530 reported by Major Cotton. If they were not then where were the records for the 350?

The testimony of survivors obtained by British Military Intelligence gives the direct lie to the official figure. Enough has already been recorded of the appalling treatment meted out to the prisoners, for commonsense and the records from other prison camps and the survivors' testimonies, to put the figure considerably higher.

We have learned that some of those who had not died of torture or starvation in one of the Alderney camps had died whilst digging out the tunnels and underground hospitals on Jersey and Guernsey. This information is supported by the testimony of Vasilli Marempolski in this book.

British Military Intelligence when reporting on the situation in Alderney and Guernsey would have been unaware of the existence of the 33 secret files and if they had, would certainly not have been permitted access to them.

Presumably acting on orders they made no attempt to verify or prove false all the rumours and stories told by those they interviewed, and as a consequence would have made no attempt to investigate the stories of prisoners, dead or alive, pushed over the cliffs.

It was twenty years later when a holiday-maker whilst diving found a huge heap of bones under the sea off the Alderney coast.

That this undeniable evidence was not discovered in the years following the liberation of the Channel Islands or was not revealed during the interrogation of prisoners found on Alderney by the British Military Intelligence is not surprising.

Only German soldiers and expendable prisoners were on the island during the occupation and all were confined to their particular camps. They were of many nationalities and most spoke only their own language so communication between many could have been difficult.

Any prisoner who 'went missing' could be accounted for by 'having been transferred for construction work to one of the other islands'. The absence of any one, or a group of prisoners, would have gone unremarked. Each man was consumed with one thought ... survival and the overriding demon of suffering was that of hunger. Day after day was filled with hours of work and pain and the ever present knowledge that should you fail to be able to work death was not far away.

The disposal into the sea would have been no problem. Heavy sea mists regularly envelope the islands, particularly Alderney, under cover of which the disposals could take place.

There are tidal races around the island of Alderney (the fastest in the world) and a knowledge of the tides flowing round the other Islands would have been useful when disposing of bodies pushed over the cliffs.

The discovery of the piles of bones would seem to provide the answer to the mystery why British Military Intelligence and the Civil Affairs Unit failed to find evidence of more than 530 deaths when they arrived on the island in 1945.

Page 10   THE DAILY MIRROR   Monday, September 1, 1939

WANTED!

FOR MURDER ... FOR KIDNAPPING ...
FOR THEFT AND FOR ARSON

ADOLF HITLER
ALIAS
Adolf Schicklegruber,
Adolf Hittler or Hidler

Last heard of in Berlin, September 3, 1939. Aged fifty, height 5ft. 8½in., dark hair, frequently brushes one lock over left forehead. Blue eyes. Sallow complexion, stout build, weighs about 11st. 3lb. Suffering from acute monomania, with periodic fits of melancholia. Frequently bursts into tears when crossed. Harsh, guttural voice, and has a habit of raising right hand to shoulder level. DANGEROUS!

FOR MURDER Wanted for the murder of over a thousand of his fellow countrymen on the night of the Blood Bath, June 30, 1934. Wanted for the murder of countless political opponents in concentration camps...

FOR KIDNAPPING Wanted for the kidnapping of Dr. Kurt Schuschnigg, late Chancellor of Austria. Wanted for the kidnapping of Pastor Niemöller...

FOR THEFT Wanted for the larceny of eighty millions of Czars gold in March, 1939. Wanted for the armed robbery of material resources of the Czech State. Wanted for the stealing of Memelland...

FOR ARSON Wanted as the incendiary who started the Reichstag fire on the night of February 27, 1933...

THIS RECKLESS CRIMINAL IS WANTED—DEAD OR ALIVE!

With this page, by Cassandra, the *Mirror* declared war on Nazi Germany. An order was issued by the German High Command that all *Mirror* directors were to be immediately arrested when London was occupied.

THE LETTERS

97 *REMAINING NAZI WAR CRIMINALS*   19:5:92

Mr David Winnick
Mr Derek Fatchett
Mr Tony Banks
Mr Alan Simpson
Mr Paul Flynn
Mrs Gwyneth Dunwoody

★ 31

Mr Bill Etherington	Mr Malcolm Chisholm	Mr John Spellar
Mr John Evans	Mr Jamie Cann	Mr Harry Barnes
Mr Jimmy Hood	Mr John McAllion	Mr Robert Hughes
Clare Short	Mr William McKelvey	(Aberdeen North)
Mr Edward O'Hara	Mr Ernie Ross	Mr John Cummings
Mr Doug Hoyle	Mr Derek Enright	Mr Peter L. Pike
Mr Max Madden	Mr Mike Watson	Mr Roy Beggs

That this House notes with approval that a notorious Nazi war criminal, Schwammberger, has just been sentenced by a German court to life imprisonment for mass murder; that amongst his numerous killings were the murder of inmates who were stripped naked on 11th September 1943, in the Przemysl camp near Krakow and shot in groups of fifty, swinging babies against walls to kill them and setting Alsatian dogs to savage inmates to death, strongly believes there can be no hiding places for such criminals and that the Syrian authorities should therefore allow Alois Brunner to be extradited to Germany to stand trial; and further believes that the British Government should now release without further delay the documents which still remain classified on the Nazi occupation of the Channel Islands and the activities at the time of Klebeck, a German citizen.

★ *The figure following this symbol gives the total number of names of Members appended, including those names added in this edition of the Notices of Questions and Motions.*

From HANSARD

Document No. 1

THE LETTERS

Monday 11 May 1992

(Answered by the Prime Minister on Monday 11 May)

UNSTARRED
No. 65
(P)

Mr David Winnick: To ask the Prime Minister, if he will state the Government's policy towards war crimes in the Channel Islands.

THE PRIME MINISTER

The Government's policy is that people who have committed murder, manslaughter or culpable homicide as violations of the laws and customs of war in German-held territory during the Second World War should not be able to use the privilege of residence in the United Kingdom, the Isle of Man or any of the Channel Islands to escape justice.

Monday 11 May 1992

(Answered by the Prime Minister on Wednesday 13 May)

UNSTARRED
No. 64
(P)

Mr David Winnick: To ask the Prime Minister, if Her Majesty's Government will now take steps to ask the German authorities to extradite Kurt Klebeck to the United Kingdom over Nazi crimes in the Channel Islands.

THE PRIME MINISTER[holding answer 11 May 1992]: Mr Klebeck is a German national. We understand that Germany does not extradite its own nationals because of a prohibition in its constitution. We would co-operate fully with the German authorities if we were asked by them for assistance in connection with any possible proceedings in Germany.

Monday 11 May 1992

(Answered by the Prime Minister on Wednesday 13 May)

UNSTARRED
No. 70
(P)

Mr David Winnick: To ask the Prime Minister, if he will now release in the public domain documents relating to the wartime Nazi occupation of the Channel Islands which remain classified; and if he will make a statement.

THE PRIME MINISTER[holding answer 11 May 1992]: Any records relating to the wartime Nazi occupation of the Channel Islands which remain closed to the public domain will be released at the appropriate time, under the criteria of the Public Records Acts of 1958 and 1967. I will however look into the matter raised by the honourable Member.

Document No. 2

63

<u>PARLIAMENTARY QUESTION FOR PRIORITY WRITTEN ANSWER</u>
<u>ON MONDAY 11TH MAY 1992</u> *Document No. 3*

QUESTION: **MR DAVID WINNICK:** To ask Mr Attorney General, if he
will make a statement on the proceedings taken by the
allies at the end of the last war against Kurt
Klebeck; and whether he will discuss with his counter-
parts in the Channel Islands the taking of proceedings
against him for Nazi War Crimes in the Channel
Islands.

MEMBER'S CONSTITUENCY: **WALSALL NORTH**   **(LAB)**

ANSWER: **MR ATTORNEY GENERAL (Rt. Hon. Sir Nicholas Lyell QC):**
No.

Kurt Klebeck was prosecuted and convicted in 1947 by
the British Military Court in Germany for

(i) being concerned in the killing of allied nationals, in
violation of the laws and usages of war, who were
interned in the Hanover/Ahnem Concentration Camp
between November 1944 and April 1945.

(ii) being concerned in the ill-treatment of allied
nationals in the same camp and during the same period
as (i) above.

He was sentenced to 10 years imprisonment.

The papers relating to the proceedings against Klebeck
are open to inspection in the Public Record Office.
I understand that he is a German national resident in
Germany. The War Crimes Act 1991 is not therefore in
issue. I further understand that Germany does not
extradite its own nationals.   The question of his
prosecution for offences alleged to have been commit-

ted in the Channel Islands is a matter for the German
authorities who have the necessary jurisdiction.

HOUSE OF COMMONS
LONDON SW1A 0AA

12th May 1992

His Excellency Baron Hermann Von Richthosen
Embassy of the Federal German Republic
23 Belgrave Square
1 Chesham Place
London
SW1X 8PZ

Your Excellency,

I am enclosing a reply which I have received from the
Attorney General regarding allegations made against Kurt
Klebeck, a German citizen, over his alledged role during the
Nazi occupation of the Channel Islands.

Your Embassy will no doubt know that The Guardian newspaper
have carried articles very recently over this matter and the
crimes that were committed by the Nazis during the
occupation of the Channel Islands.

Since it is not apparently the policy of your Government to
extradite its own nationals to stand trial for alledged
crimes, I do trust that the prosecution authorities in
Germany will give very serious consideration to the
allegations which have been made against Klebeck. I hope
you will agree that it would be totally unacceptable that
those who have committed crimes against humanity should go
scott free simply because of the lapse in time involved.

As of course you will know, the British Parliament passed
the War Crimes Act in order to try and ensure that those who
now reside in Britain and who alledgedly committed Nazi
crimes during the war can be tried, but this would not
affect someone living outside the UK.

I look forward to your reply.

Yours sincerely,

David Winnick

Document No. 4

DER BOTSCHAFTER
DER BUNDESREPUBLIK DEUTSCHLAND
THE AMBASSADOR
OF THE FEDERAL REPUBLIC OF GERMANY

Baron Hermann von Richthofen

London, 1 June 1992

Dear Mr. Winnick,

Thank you very much for your letters of 12 and 21 May 1992 concerning Mr. Klebeck's alleged role during the German occupation of the Channel Islands.

As the Attorney General has already pointed out in Parliament the Federal Republic of Germany does not extradite its own nationals. It is bound by article 16 para 2 of the Basic Law which reads: "No German may be extradited to a foreign country." However, any German can be brought to trial in Germany by the Public Prosecutor if there is sufficient proof for the alleged crimes.

I am sure that also in the case of Kurt Klebeck the German prosecution authorities will give very serious consideration to the allegations against this man once the incriminating material has been made available to them.

I have brought your letters and a similar one from Mr. Greville Janner to the attention of the Federal Foreign Office.

Yours sincerely
Hermann von Richthofen

Mr. David Winnick, MP
House of Commons
London SW1A OAA

Document No. 5

THE LETTERS

HOUSE OF COMMONS
LONDON SW1A 0AA

3rd August 1992

The Rt Hon John Major MP
Prime Minister
10 Downing Street
London
SW1

Dear Prime Minister,

On the 13th May you answered a Parliamentary Question of
mine regarding releasing in the public domain documents
relating to the war-time Nazi occupation of the Channel
Islands which remain classified (unstarred No.70). In your
answer you stated that records relating to the occupation
which remain closed to the public domain will be released at
the appropriate time, under the criteria of the Public
Records Act 1958 and 1967. You added, however, that you
would look into the matter further.

I am now enclosing an article from The Mail on Sunday which
is based apparently on documents which are not due to be
released until 2045. The article shows the extent of Nazi
brutality and murders which occurred at the time.

I do hope that the Government will now accept that documents
relating to the occupation of the Channel Islands should now
be officially brought into the public domain, and there is
no longer any real reason why forty-seven years since the
war ended such papers should remain classified and for so
many more years to come.

I am letting it be known that I have written to you.

Yours sincerely,

Dictated by David Winnick
and signed in his absence

Document No. 6

Document No. 7

10 DOWNING STREET
LONDON SW1A 2AA

THE PRIME MINISTER

7 August 1992

1 Jac / David,

    I promised in my reply to your written Parliamentary
Question on 13 May to look into the matter which you raised
concerning the release into the public domain of documents
relating to the wartime Nazi occupation of the Channel Islands.
Thank you too for your letter of 3 August. I am looking into the
significance, if any, of the article from the Mail on Sunday
which you enclosed.

    As you know, the Public Records Acts established criteria
under which such documents are withheld until it is appropriate
for them to be released. I have now asked William Waldegrave,
as part of his work on openness in government, to consult the
Lord Chancellor, as Minister with responsibility for the Public
Records Acts, on the operation in practice of those criteria.
The purpose of such an exercise will be to ensure that only those
papers which are properly identified as possessing the necessary
sensitivity are withheld from the public domain.

    I should emphasise that the policy of the Government is to
release rather than to retain records wherever possible. To this
end, departments are constantly reviewing the continuing
sensitivity of their files to see whether further records may be
made available. The Home Office are, for example, currently

reviewing their files relating to the German occupation of the
Channel Islands.

Your Sincerely,

John M.

David Winnick Esq MP

68

THE GUARDIAN
Tuesday August 11 1992

Document No. 8

Death camp papers may be released

Madeleine Bunting

HOME Office files which may shed light on collaboration and the use of slave labour during the Nazi occupation of the Channel Islands may be released next month.

The Home Office said 500 files — which have been classified for 75 to 100 years — are under review and a large part of them is expected to be released within six weeks.

The Prime Minister, replying to a letter from David Winnick, Labour MP for Walsall — who has led a parliamentary campaign for the files to be released — said yesterday the Home Office was reviewing the files.

"Only those papers which are properly identified as possessing the necessary sensitivity are withheld," John Major said in his letter.

"I should emphasise that the government policy is to release rather than to retain records wherever possible. To this end departments are constantly reviewing the continuing sensitivity of their files to see whether further records can be made available."

Brian Wilson, Labour's Citizen's Charter spokesman, welcomed the review. "It would be a major breakthrough in the opening up of this period if the files were to be released. Continued secrecy in this field serves only to protect those whose records and reputations are unworthy of public scrutiny."

In May the Guardian published details of an SS death camp on Alderney and told of the brutal treatment of Russian slave labourers and the extent of islanders' collaboration with the Germans. Since then, the Government has come under increased pressure from historians and MPs to release files.

The review move comes in the wake of a report at the weekend that William Waldegrave, the minister responsible for the Citizen's Charter, has asked the Lord Chancellor, Lord Mackay, to review the system determining which government documents are subject to the 30-year secrecy rule. Mr Waldegrave will publish a white paper at the end of the year.

The occupation files could shed light on the investigations of the Civil Affairs Unit which accompanied the allied forces onto the islands in May 1945. The unit investigated collaboration and concluded that "a number of people acted in an unseemly, undesirable or even disgraceful way", according to documents in the Public Record Office.

The unit passed on 12 cases to the Director of Public Prosecutions who agreed that there was prima facie evidence of "conduct of highly reprehensible and even possibly disloyal nature".

No case came to trial because the Defence of the Realm Act, under which collaboration was a crime, had been abrogated in the Channel Islands in 1943.

The files could also provide more information on whether profits made during the occupation from selling food and supplies to the Germans were effectively taxed — a matter of controversy in the Channel Islands to this day.

The files will be not be released if there is a security consideration or if they are personally sensitive for people still alive, or possibly for their descendants, a Home Office spokesman said.

Mr Winnick said his campaign to bring to trial one of the commandants of the Alderney SS death camp, Kurt Klebeck, now living in Hamburg, would continue.

The newspaper article referred to in David Winnick's letter on page 65: Document 4.

HOUSE OF COMMONS
LONDON SW1A 0AA

11th August 1992

His Excellency Baron Hermann von Richthofen
The Ambassador of the Federal Republic of Germany
23 Belgrave Square
London
SW1X 8PZ

Your Excellency

Thank you for your letter of 1st June regarding Klebeck.

You informed me that the prosecution authorities in your
country will be giving very serious consideration to the
allegations against this person for alleged war crimes
against humanity. I would be pleased if you could let me
know the latest position in this matter and I am enclosing a
copy of a newspaper report in today's Guardian which, as you
will see, shows that quite a number of documents relating to
the war-time occupation of the Channel Islands could well be
released in the near future.

However, I assume that the prosecution authorities in
Germany will have considerable data on Klebeck, without the
British documents, and bearing in mind Klebeck's alleged
role in other concentration camps apart from the Channel
Islands.

Yours sincerely

David Winnick

Dictated by David Winnick
and signed in his absence

Document No. 9

THE LETTERS

Botschaft
der Bundesrepublik Deutschland
Embassy
of the Federal Republic of Germany
Az.: RK 530.00
(Please quote ref.)

London, 20 August 1992
Oe/wg

Direct Line: 071 824 1450

Mr. David Winnick, MP
House of Commons
London SW1A 0AA

L   ⌐

Dear Mr. Winnick,

Ambassador von Richthofen has asked me to thank you for your
letter of 11 August 1992 regarding Kurt Klebeck.

The Federal Ministry of Justice has asked the Public Prosecutor of
Hamburg to report whether their previous investigations against
Klebeck has ever included incidents at the labour camp in Alderney
and his alleged responsibility for the death of 350 prisoners. It
has also passed on copies of your previous letters and the
articles published by the British press on Klebeck's role as
commander of the camps on Alderney to the above Hamburg authority.

As soon as I get further information on the matter I shall let you
know.

Yours sincerely,

B. Oetter
Consul General

Document No. 10

Adresse:
23, Belgrave Square/Chesham Place
London, SW1X 8PZ

Post:

Telefon:
071-235 5033
071-824 1300

Telefax:
071-235 0609

Telex:
21650
Kennung:
AALDNE G

BT211

Chancellor of the Duchy of Lancaster
Minister of Public Service and Science

CABINET OFFICE
70 Whitehall, London SW1A 2AS
Telephone: 071-270 0400

David Winnick Esq MP
House of Commons
London SW1A OAA

19 September 1992

Dear David

Thank you for your letter of 7 September.

The review of papers relating to the wartime occupation of the Channel Islands, to which the Prime Minister referred in his letter to you of 7 August, is being carried out by the Home Office. I understand that the review is due to be completed in October and that there will be an announcement prior to the release of material which is found to be no longer sensitive. I am sending a copy of your letter to Kenneth Clarke who will I am sure let you have any further information there may be on this.

The second paragraph of the Prime Minister's letter refers to a more general review of the criteria under which documents are withheld in accordance with the provisions of the Public Records Acts. It was about this review that, at the Prime Minister's request, I consulted the Lord Chancellor as the Minister responsible for the Public Records Acts. In the context of the Government's policy on more open government the Lord Chancellor has agreed to carry out a review of the operation in practice of the criteria to ensure that only those documents which are deemed truly sensitive continue to be withheld from the public domain. The outcome will be announced when the review has been completed.

William

WILLIAM WALDEGRAVE

Document No. 11

72

THE LETTERS

Monday, 30 November 1992

Written No. 65

Mr David Winnick (Walsall North): To ask the Secretary
of State for the Home Department, pursuant to his
Answer of 6 November, Official Report, column 528, when
he will be making a statement regarding his
Department's records relating to the wartime Nazi
occupation of the Channel Islands.

MR KENNETH CLARKE

[holding answer 27 November 1992]

The review of files relating to this period has been
completed and most of the files will now be opened to
public scrutiny. The Ministry of Defence will continue
to hold a small number of files on extended closure under
section 5(1) of the Public Record Act 1958 on the grounds
of personal sensitivity. The Home Office will also hold
a few records on extended closures. Other records being
released by the Home Office will be available for public
inspection at the Public Record Office, Kew from Tuesday,
1 December.   *Document No. 12*

CHANNEL ISLANDS: RELEASE OF HOME OFFICE PAPERS RELATING TO THE
WARTIME NAZI OCCUPATION

The Home Office will announce on 30 November that the review of
Home Office papers relating to the wartime Nazi occupation of
the Channel Islands is complete.   The end result is that the
Home Office is only holding 7 files on extended closure under
section 5(1) of the Public Record Act 1958.   The vast majority
of files will be opened to public inspection however, including
16 files where information has been extracted from certain
documents because of personal sensitivity, or in two instances
on the grounds of national security.

Document No. 13

THE LETTERS

HOUSE OF COMMONS
LONDON SW1A 0AA

David Winnick MP
House of Commons
London SW1A 0AA

2 December 1992

Dear Mr Winnick,

Re: Nazi occupation of the Channel Islands

You asked me to identify the issues that are still "live".

We are exploring whether there is any information that is still withheld which substantiates allegations of war crimes committed by Channel Islands residents or German officers. We know that there are seven files withheld by the Home Office under section 5(1) of the Public Records Act 1958 (Home Office Press briefing 1 December 1992 - copy enclosed). We also know that a further "small number of files" are being withheld by the Ministry of Defence (from the Home Secretary's answer to your written Parliamentary Question of 30 November).

We do not know whether such files contain any information about allegations of war crimes or atrocities committed on Alderney by either UK or non-UK citizens. Neither do we know whether any of these papers would be usefully submitted to prosecuting authorities in this country or in Germany.

I believe that Greville Janner is planning to submit written PQs based on these issues.

Finally, I understand that you have been corresponding with the German authorities about Kurt Klebeck. Has there been any movement on whether they are investigating allegations against him? I would be grateful for any news.

Yours sincerely,

Jeremy Coleman
ASSISTANT SECRETARY

Document No. 14

HOUSE OF COMMONS
LONDON SW1A 0AA

3rd December 1992

Rt Hon Kenneth Clarke QC MP
Secretary of State
Home Office
50 Queen Anne's Gate
London
SW1H 9AT

Dear Home Secretary,

I am pleased of course that a large number of documents relating to the Nazi wartime occupation of the Channel Islands have now been released.

However, I am somewhat concerned that there does not seem to be amongst the released documents any relating to the camps on Alderney. As you will know, many Nazi crimes were committed in these camps and perhaps you could let me know if these are amongst the documents which have been held back.

I am also writing to Malcolm Rifkind.

Yours sincerely,

David Winnick

Document No. 15

3rd December 1992

Rt Hon Malcolm Rifkind QC MP
Secretary of State
Ministry of Defence
Main Building
Whitehall
London
SW1A 2HB

Dear Secretary of State,

I am enclosing a copy of a letter which I have written to
Kenneth Clarke regarding the release of documents over the
Nazi wartime occupation of the Channel Islands.

I would be pleased if you could let me know if your
Department holds any documents relating to the camps on
Alderney. I understand, and perhaps you will let me know if
this is so, that some of the records over Alderney were
passed to the Soviet authorities at the end of the war. If
this is the case, perhaps in the new political climate the
Russians could be asked what action they took or will be
taking regarding the Nazi crimes on Alderney, and bearing in
mind that a large number of Russians were done to death
there.

Yours sincerely,

David Winnick

Document No. 16

MINISTER OF STATE FOR THE ARMED FORCES

TUESDAY 8 DECEMBER 1992

MR DAVID WINNICK (LABOUR)(WALSALL NORTH)

73	Mr Winnick	To ask the Secretary of State for Defence, what documents his Department holds relating to the wartime Nazi crimes in the camps on Alderney in the Channel Islands, and if any such records have been given to the former Soviet authorities.
P		

MR ARCHIE HAMILTON

The Ministry of Defence does not hold any relevant papers. Detailed records of the British investigations into WWII war crimes in the Channel Islands are available for public examination at the Public Record Office.

Copies of records relating to the investigations into the incidents on Alderney and Jersey were passed to the former Soviet Authorities in October 1945.

Ministry of Defence

8 December 1992

Document No. 17

THE LETTERS

MINISTRY OF DEFENCE
MAIN BUILDING WHITEHALL LONDON SW1A 2HB
Telephone 071-21 .... (Direct Dialling)
071-21 89000 (Switchboard)

PARLIAMENTARY UNDER-SECRETARY OF STATE
FOR DEFENCE

D/US of S RMC 1973   8 January 1993

Dear Mr. Winnick,

Thank you for your letter of 3 December, to Malcolm Rifkind,
about the wartime Nazi crimes in the camps on Alderney.

You will now have seen, from Archie Hamilton's reply to your
Parliamentary Question of 8 December, (Hansard, Col 614) that
the Ministry of Defence does not hold any relevant papers, and
that copies of records relating to the investigations into the
incidents on Alderney and Jersey were passed to the former
Soviet Authorities in October 1945.

As far as we are aware, the Russians took no action on those
documents, but you will doubtless also have noted, from Archie
Hamilton's and Kenneth Clarke's replies to questions from
Greville Janner, on 10 December (Hansard Cols 799 and 741), that
MOD and Home Office policy and practice is to make the Channel
Islands War Crimes paper available to the official prosecuting
authority with the responsibility of investigating alleged War
Crimes.

I appreciate your concern for those who suffered from the events
in the Channel Islands and in this connection, you will, I am
sure, be interested to hear that the German Authorities, who
have jurisdiction in this matter, have now begun their own
investigations into these incidents, with particular regard to
I appreciate your concern for those who suffered from the events
in the Channel Islands and in this connection, you will, I am
sure, be interested to hear that the German Authorities, who
have jurisdiction in this matter, have now begun their own
investigations into these incidents, with particular regard to
the role played by Kurt Klebeck. The German Authorities have
been in touch with my Officials about the examination of
relevant papers and the Ministry of Defence, along with other
Departments, will be giving every assistance with the
investigations in this direction.

As far as the Russian Authorities are concerned, any follow-up
action is, of course, for them to decide. I do not feel that it
is for us to press this matter with them.

I hope this is helpful. I am copying this letter to Kenneth
Clarke.

Yours sincerely,

Robert Cranborne

David Winnick Esq MP

79

HOUSE OF COMMONS
LONDON SW1A 0AA

12th January 1993

His Excellency Baron Hermann von Richthofen
The Ambassador of the Federal Republic of Germany
23 Belgrave Square
London
SW1X 8PZ

Your Excellency,

The Consul General at the Embassy replied on the 20th August
last year to my letter of the 1st June regarding Klebeck and
his role during the Nazi occupation of the Channel Islands.

I would be pleased if you could let me know the latest
position over this matter, and if the Public Prosecutor of
Hamburg has reported yet over Klebeck's role at the camps in
Alderney where many deaths of prisoners took place.

As you will no doubt know, the authorities in Guernsey last
week released further documents regarding the occupation and
I am enclosing a reply which I have received from the
Parliamentary Under-Secretary of State for Defence which has
some relevance in this matter. I note that your authorities
have been in touch with Ministry of Defence officials over
the examination of various papers and I am of course pleased
about this.

Yours sincerely,

David Winnick

Document No. 19

THE LETTERS

Thursday, 14 January 1993

Written No. 62

Mr David Winnick (Walsall North): To ask the Secretary
of State for the Home Department, pursuant to his
Answer of 30 November 1992, Official Report, columns
7-8, what account he took, during his review concerning
the wartime occupation of the Channel Islands, of the
documents held by the authorities in Jersey; and if he
will make a statement.

MR KENNETH CLARKE

None. The Jersey records are not subject to the
United Kingdom Public Records Acts and do not come within
my responsibilities. Any decision relating to them is
wholly a matter for the Jersey authorities.

Document No. 20

HOME OFFICE
QUEEN ANNE'S GATE
LONDON SW1H 9AT

Our Ref: MLA/92 6/6/2
           PO 26767/92

19 JAN 1993

Thank you for your letter of 3 December to the Home Secretary about
the release of documents relating to the Nazi wartime occupation of
the Channel Islands.

I am afraid there is very little I can add to the answer already
given by the Home Secretary to the question raised by
Greville Janner on 10 December, at Hansard column 741. A recent
development is that the Home Office has now received a request from
the German judicial authorities for the production of information
relating to allegations of crimes committed on the Channel Islands
during World War II by persons working for the occupying
German authorities. The lead department for coordinating the
handling of all such requests is the Ministry of Defence, and my
officials will be making available all documents whether open or
closed.

MICHAEL JACK

David Winnick Esq MP

Document No. 21

HOUSE OF COMMONS
LONDON SW1A 0AA

21st January 1993

Sir Peter Crill CBE
Bailiff
Bailiff Chambers
Royal Square
St Helier
Jersey
Channel Islands

Dear Sir Peter,

I am writing to you regarding records dealing with the Nazi
war-time occupation of Jersey. As you will know, the Home
Office very recently made available most of the records
relating to the Channel Islands during the last week and
Guernsey did so as well shortly afterwards.

I would be pleased if you could let me know if it is also
intended for the Jersey records to be released in full. I
would very much hope so and bearing in mind what the Home
Office and the authorities in Guernsey have already done.

Yours sincerely,

David Winnick

Document No. 22

The Bailiff of Jersey
Sir Peter Crill, C.B.E.

THE BAILIFF'S CHAMBERS
ROYAL COURT HOUSE
JERSEY JE1 1DD

Your Ref

Our Ref   O 4

Tel: (0534) 502100

Fax: (0534) 502199

25th January, 1993

Dear Mr. Winnick,

      Thank you for your letter of the 21st January, 1993, about the Island records dealing with the Nazi wartime Occupation of Jersey.

      I believe that Insular Authorities are willing to release the archives but there are two difficulties.

1.   They have not been collated under the charge of an archivist. It is only recently that the States have agreed to set up an Archivist Service.

2.   Some of the archives from this department of Bailiff Coutanche, not only of the Occupation years but immediately afterwards, were stolen in 1991. Most of them, fortunately, were recovered but the Police are retaining them because they wish to use them as evidence against a number of people who, 'I am told, are likely to be prosecuted for receiving. The principal thieves have been tried and convicted.

      Until, therefore, we have an archivist who can gather the various documents and sort them out in a proper fashion, the practical difficulties will remain for anyone wishing to see a particular item.

      Having said that most of the relevant papers were seen by Professor Charles Cruikshank who wrote the official history of the Occupation for the Trustees of the Imperial War Museum. As regards the Occupation and the conduct of the Channel Island Authorities of the day, you may have seen my letter to the Times which was published last Saturday. In case you missed it I enclose a copy.

      Should you require any further information, or if there is any way in which I can help you if you are thinking of doing researches here, please let me know.

      Yours sincerely,

Bailiff

D. Winnick, Esq., MP,
House of Commons,
LONDON SW1A 0AA

Document No. 23

THE LETTERS

MINISTRY OF DEFENCE
MAIN BUILDING WHITEHALL LONDON SW1A 2HB

Telephone 071-21 .... (Direct Dialling)
071-21 89000 (Switchboard)

PARLIAMENTARY UNDER-SECRETARY OF STATE
FOR DEFENCE

D/US of S/RMC 16/1/4   5 February 1993

Dear Mr Winnick,

Knowing of your interest in the matter of war crimes committed by
the Germans in the Channel Islands during WW2, I would like to
advise you of my intentions with regard to the few MOD files
concerned with the Channel Islands during this period which have
not yet been released to the public domain.

Once the files have been considered by the German authorities
looking into the question of German war crimes in the Channel
Islands, we will be releasing the files in the Public Record
Office. I will let you know when the files are ready for
release.

Yours sincerely,

Robert Cranborne

The Viscount Cranborne

David Winnick Esq MP

Recycled Paper

Document No. 24

85

MINISTRY OF DEFENCE
MAIN BUILDING WHITEHALL LONDON SW1A 2HB

Telephone 071-21 .... (Direct Dialling)
071-21 89000 (Switchboard)

PARLIAMENTARY UNDER-SECRETARY OF STATE
FOR DEFENCE

D/US of S RMC 16/1/4   17 February 1993

Dear Mr. Winnick,

Thank you for your letter of 4 February concerning the future
release of the few MOD files relating to the Channel Islands in
World War II that are not available in the public domain.

I feel I should clear up in advance of their release a
misunderstanding as to their general nature. The papers
concerned cover the debriefing by the Military Intelligence
organisation during, rather than at the end of the war, of
personnel who had information on the Channel Islands. Such
people were debriefed with the primary intention of obtaining
the maximum amount of intelligence data on the German garrison's
organisation, strength and defences on the Channel Islands that
might oppose any British landing attempt.

Therefore, contrary to media reports, they were not part of the
War Office's post-liberation war crimes investigations. The
papers of the latter are, as you know, already in the public
domain in the PRO at Kew and have been for some years.

I am copying this letter to Greville Janner.

Yours Sincerely,

Robert Cranborne.

The Viscount Cranborne

David Winnick Esq MP

Recycled Paper

Document No. 25

THE LETTERS

TUESDAY 15 JUNE 1993

MR DAVID WINNICK (LABOUR)(WALSALL NORTH)

44	Mr Winnick	To ask the Secretary of State for
P		Defence, if he will make a statement

To ask the Secretary of State for
Defence, if he will make a statement
on the release of any further
documents relating to the wartime
Nazi occupation of the Channel
Islands; and what inspection of
these documents have been undertaken
by representatives of the German
authorities.

MR HANLEY

The majority of MOD documents relating to the
wartime Nazi occupation of the Channel Islands are already
in the public domain. The German authorities are examining
all MOD documents relating to this matter. When they have
completed this task those files currently closed will be
opened for public inspection at the Public Record Office.

Ministry of Defence
15 June 1993

Document No. 26

87

DER BOTSCHAFTER
DER BUNDESREPUBLIK DEUTSCHLAND
THE AMBASSADOR
OF THE FEDERAL REPUBLIC OF GERMANY

Dr. Peter Hartmann

London, 18 November 1993

Dear Mr. Winnick,

Referring to your letter of 4 November 1993 concerning the case of the German national Kurt Klebeck, under suspicion of alleged war crimes during the Second World War on the Channel Islands, I would like to inform you that the Prosecution Service in Hamburg has opened an enquiry into these allegations. The enquiry is based on the documentation presented to the Federal Ministry of Justice on the Federal Republic of Germany by the British Ministry of Defence - Army Historical Branch - in May 1993 after a request by the German authorities of 6 November 1992.

I am not in a position to comment on the further course of the enquiry for this is now a strictly judicial matter.

Yours sincerely,

Mr.
David Winnick, MP
House of Commons
London SW1A 0AA

Document No. 27

THE LETTERS

MINISTER OF STATE FOR THE ARMED FORCES

TUESDAY 23 NOVEMBER 1993

MR DAVID WINNICK (LABOUR)(WALSALL NORTH)

12	Mr Winnick	To ask the Secretary of State for
N		Defence, if he will make a statement over remaining documents in his Department relating to the Nazi occupation of the Channel Islands; and if such documents have now been seen by the German authorities.

MR HANLEY

There are very few closed documents relating to the Nazi occupation of the Channel Islands. The German authorities' investigations are proceeding with MOD giving every assistance, including sight of the relevant files. The closed documents will be released on completion of the German enquiries.

Note by the Author:
If as stated in the first line of this letter "there are very few closed documents relating to the Nazi Occupation" then to what do the 'closed documents' refer?

Ministry of Defence

23 November 1993

Document No. 28

J'Accuse

To the two questions put to the Prime Minister on Wednesday 11th May 1992 and answered by him on the 11th and 13th May 1992, Mr. Winnick received the following reply: "We understand that Germany does not extradite its own nationals because of a prohibition in its constitution. We would co-operate fully with the German authorities if we were asked by them for assistance in connection with any proceedings in Germany".

What a pitifully weak response! How naive! Is it likely that the German Authorities would voluntarily bring to justice German nationals accused of atrocities in the Second World War? They would surely do everything possible to shelter such men. A glance at the picture of the OdR Bearers Association meeting on page {...} tells it all.

The Prime Minister's reply to the second question was equally evasive and vague 'The Government's policy is that people who have committed murder, manslaughter or culpable homicide as violations of the laws and customs of war in German-held territory (i.e. most of Europe including the Channel Islands) during the Second World War should not be able to use the privileges of residence in the United Kingdom, the Isle of Man or any of the Channel Islands to escape justice".

Would they want to do so when they can escape to Germany and remain safe there?

It is known that Werner von Braun, the scientist behind the V1 and V2 rockets which killed and wounded over 20,000 people in London was given safe haven in the United States and that SS Colonel Professor Dr Frank Six who was responsible for wholesale massacres in the Soviet Union was released after four years of his 20 year sentence.

Evil men are still roaming free in this country. They are not so important as Braun or Six, but should they be allowed to remain free in the light of the Prime Minister's reply to the second question? How pro-German is the Establishment?

Were the investigating personnel as naive as they seemed?

Prisoners working on the fortifications and tunnels in Jersey and Guernsey when they became too weak to work or too ill, were returned to Alderney and then transported to Neuengamme where they were expected to die.

But were they all returned Neuengamme? Why bother? They were of no further use to the Germans. They were a liability; a strain on food supplies, so why not dispose of them into the sea?

Once again referral to the pattern of German behaviour during the war and treatment of concentration camp inmates points to a policy of the easiest cheapest method of disposal.

The question of a humane approach never arose.

Because Vassili Marempolski, although unfit for further work, was still mobile he was destined for Neuengamme. This saved his life. As a numeral on the records he appears as a 'transportation' figure. He escaped but had he stayed and arrived at Neuengamme he would have been dead within weeks.

In 'The Rise and Fall of the Third Reich; A History of Nazi Germany' (London: Secker & Warburg 1961) the author William Shirer described 'The Black Book' as **'among the more amusing 'invasion' documents'**. 'The Rise and Fall' is an excellent book, and should be read.

There is however an unwitting, perhaps unconscious, revelation in the use of the phrase 'among the more amusing 'invasion' documents'. This is underlined by the following ... "although 'The Black Book' abounds with **howlers** (the emphasis is the author's) and obvious inaccuracies" a comment found in the last paragraph of the Introduction.

These are the remarks which might be found in a schoolboy essay and serve to highlight the attitude of mind in the ruling and administrative classes in Whitehall before, during and since the war.

They are comments of the kind made by people cocooned from reality with closed minds, unable to see the true pattern of life. It is an arrogance, a disregard, or a refusal, to see the truth because it does not (as discussed elsewhere) fit preconceived concepts.

However, 'The Black Book' amusing and inaccurate as it may be in the eyes of some has a chilling message for those prepared to accept it for what it was intended ... the 'net' into which would be drawn the most famous, talented people of our community who were known by the Nazis to have been or have expressed anti-Hitler, anti-Nazi, anti-Fascist ideas. The man who would have headed arrest operations in Britain would have been SS Colonel Professor Dr Frank Six. His Headquarters were to have been in London (if London had not by then been flattened). Before joining the SS Six had been the Dean of the Economic Faculty at Berlin University. Interesting evidence of the two sides of the German character.

Under his command would have been six 'Einsatzkommandos' (Action Commandos) the sub-headquarters would have been London, Birmingham, Bristol, Edinburgh, Liverpool and Manchester.

The discovery of 'The Black Book' did a number of things:-

1) It proved the intention of Hitler, sooner or later, to make war on Britain, long before war was declared.

2) It demonstrated that compilation of the list must have commenced some years before the outbreak of war because of the omissions and inclusions of various names and that it was updated in 1940.

3) It proved that German Intelligence was very well informed on day to day life in Britain and the individuals involved.

4) It underlined the argument offered on page 42 that the German approach to any problem is meticulous.

5) The presence of so few Military personnel in the list would seem to indicate the existence of another list and this is confirmed by the order issued by the German High Command that all *'Mirror'* directors were to be arrested (and no doubt eventually executed) when London was occupied.

6) Heydrich had ordered the preparation of The Black List and it dealt largely with Political, Jewish and Civilian individuals (see list at back of book).

7) In the introduction to *'The Black Book'* we are told it was compiled in May 1940 by Walter Schellenberg, Chief of Amt (Bureau) IVE of the RSHA (Reichssicherheitshauptamt) the Bureau responsible for counter-espionage.

8) There is a small discrepancy in this statement. Whilst it was no doubt brought up to date in 1940 and edited by Walter Schellenberg a careful examination of the names in the list indicates it was begun years before war was declared

9) The official name of *'The Black Book'* is ... ...

   'The SONDERFAHNDUNGSLISTE G.B.' which interpreted is *'Special Search List GB'*

10) It is understandable that the militant anti-Nazi *'Daily Mirror'* would have been the responsibility of the German Military. (See page 60 for the reason why).

For the most appalling atrocities committed in the Soviet Union Six was sentenced in 1948 at the Nuremburg trials as a war criminal to 20 years imprisonment but was released only 4 years later by the American, British and German Authorities to work in the West German Intelligence Service alongside a number of Gestapo and SS members to spy on the Soviet Union.

The fact that the SS had been identified as a criminal organisation and therefore all members were considered criminal was apparently ignored.

Was this the reconstruction of a nation to which Lord Annan referred?

Six then, is the man who would have decided the fate of Churchill, Beaverbrook, Peter Ustinov, Noel Coward and thousands more dear to the hearts of the British public.

Hitler decided on 17th September 1939 to create an overall directorate with SS Obergruppenfuhrer Reinhard Heydrich at its head for the purpose of controlling Reich Security.

The RSHA (Reichssicherheitshauptamt) was to be divided into seven bureaux covering absolutely every aspect of life in a civil society including the planned destruction of that Society.

It is not the purpose of this book to list in detail the activities assigned to each bureau (AMT), sufficient to say that the whole presents a spine-chilling picture, nor shall we here attempt to list all the 2820 people named for arrest and presumably prison and extermination in Jersey and or Guernsey.

Among the 2820 were politicians, titled people who had not been afraid to express publicly their disapproval of the Nazi regime, and of course journalists and newspaper proprietors who had used their media to oppose Hitler. There were artists, actors, composers, musicians, industrialists and left-wing expressionists.

As the net closed in and records, documents and information obtained under interrogation revealed even more names the 2820 in the original 'Black Book' list would have swelled into many more thousands.

Not only all the Directors of the 'Daily Mirror', which had set the lead in condemning the Nazi Movement in Germany and Hitler, but such men as William Neil Connor (better known as Cassandra the famous columnist of the time) and Richard Jennings the Leader writer, must have been on the 'arrest' list.

It is interesting that they do not appear in 'The Black Book' confirming the fact that arrests would not have stopped at 3000.

One of the prominent names not included in 'The Black Book' for a different reason was David Lloyd George, the former British Prime Minister. In an article published in the 'Daily Express' of 17th November 1936 he wrote:

"I have now seen the famous German leader and also something of the great change he has effected. Whatever one may think of his methods – and they are certainly not those of a parliamentary party – there can be no doubt that he has achieved a marvellous transformation in the spirit of the people"

In the same year he had said of Hitler ...

"He is indeed a great man. Fuhrer is the proper name for him, for he is a born leader – yes, a statesman".

Also absent from 'The Black Book' list is George Bernard Shaw. Unlike many other British writers his plays and writings were published and performed in Nazi Germany and on 7th October 1939 issue of the 'New Statesman' he wrote of Hitler ...

"Our business is to make peace with him and with all the world instead of making more mischief and ruining our people in the process".

Frequently in disagreement with her father's views it is not surprising that Lloyd George's daughter Megan Lloyd George **does** appear in 'The Black Book', surely, once and for all disproving the suggestion by some writers and Military and Civil Authorities that 'The Black Book' is one great big laugh.

Also on 'The Black Book' list was Sefton Delmer, Paris representative of the 'Daily Express'. Himmler, whose Security Services was made responsible for preparing the list must have included Sefton Delmer with some relish for it was he who had criticised, in one of his broadcasts, Hitler's 1940 Reichstag speech.

Evidently anticipating the possibility of defeat in 1940 Harold Nicholson, Parliamentary Secretary to the Ministry of Information told his wife he had obtained a 'suicide' pill which they could take if the worst happened.

Over 150 names have been selected from the list of 2820 and these appear as an appendix to this book.

Also listed in 'The Black Book' are the addresses of the Branches of the Labour Party and other leftist groups. Trades Union Headquarters are listed and their branch addresses throughout the country, and, as mentioned elsewhere the Grand Lodge of England would have been visited.

Newspapers, Businesses, Associations, Public Services, Banks, Universities, nothing is left out.

Adding willingly to the list and no doubt, providing access to their own records would have been the many pro-Nazi, anti-semitic, pro-Fascist personalities in positions of influence.

In the years before the war Sir Oswald Mosley and his Blackshirt Movement attempted to emulate in Britain the successes of Hitler's Brownshirts in Germany.

The same 'heil' salute was adopted and the uniforms were a copy of the SS. Much of their activity was confined to the poorer parts of the big Cities including, of course, the East End of London. The degree of support they received was not inconsiderable, for one of the main features of their 'gospel' was of course anti-semitism. A list of 'wanted' Jews was compiled.

Contrary to the general impression, probably deliberately circulated, the active followers of the Blackshirt Movement were not all trouble seekers, out-of-work, 'rent-a-mob' bullies but a high percentage were from the middle and upper classes. This fact is confirmed by close examination of the Pathé News films taken of the Blackshirt activities, marches and clashes with anti-Fascist and Left-wing organisations.

Protests were raised that whereas Left-wing/Anti-Fascist marches were strictly controlled or banned too much freedom was given to Sir Oswald Mosley's Fascist Party in much the same way that Unionist Marches are permitted and protected in Northern Ireland whilst Nationalists events are strictly controlled.

The culmination of Blackshirt activities was reached with a planned march into the East End of London, the intention being a 'pogrom' of the Jewish community. Alerted to this, the Jewish community were able to organise their defences. Streets were barricaded and the ensuing fight became known as the Cable Street Riots. So fierce was the fighting the police, who had seemed to favour the Blackshirt activities, were forced to surrender and retired. As a result of this incident Fascist Party marches were banned. All this before the war. Finally Sir Oswald Mosley was interned for the duration of the war.

All these events, some secretly and unlawfully, were filmed by Pathé News and after the war by TV-News sources and could be seen in the Documentary 'Forbidden Britain' shown on BBC2 Television on Thursday 17th November 1994.

In the same documentary it is stated that the membership of Sir Oswald Mosley's Fascist Party reached well over 150,000 thus providing a nationwide network of cooperation to be called upon and brought into action when the Nazis had defeated Britain.

There is perhaps cause for concern amongst those wishing to defend the minority groups, in the apparent reluctance of various members of the Establishment and the Armed Forces to bring to justice the Nazi/Fascists still at large in our midst.

The question arises, how many people would prefer a Fascist regime to a true Democracy? It is a question very relevant in the years prior to the war and equally relevant today.

It should be remembered that before the war the influx of coloured people had not yet occured, when it did in the 1950s, Mosley's Blackshirts switched their persecution to the minority ethnic races, and seem still to pursue that policy under the title of National Front supported by a branch of the organisation involved in personal violence under the title of Combat 18.

From time to time Sir Oswald Mosley received the support of the 'Daily Mail' in publicising the activities of the Blackshirt Movement. This might be interpreted as an oblique public statement by the paper that it was **not** 'leftist' and a dig at the 'Daily Mirror', for, as has been remarked elsewhere, in the decade leading up to the war there was the 'apparent' stark choice between Communism and Fascism.

In January 1934 a Major Yeats-Brown who was known to have pro-Fascist leanings founded the January Club. Its creation had the express purpose of interesting influential people in the aims of the Blackshirt Movement, following a pattern which had proved effective in the rise to power of the National Socialist party in Germany when the rise of Communism was feared there.

It is now common knowledge that MI5 had been monitoring all these activities since the inception of the Blackshirts.

One of the persons regularly attending the Club dinners was Mr G Ward-Price, a director of Associated Newspapers.

In a secret MI5 report not released until 1983, many distinguished guests of the times are named as having attended one or another of the January Club dinners.

Perhaps the significance of the choice of January as a title and a month in which to launch the Club was not lost upon MI5.

No doubt one of its more classically inclined members remembered that it was Numa Pompilius, a legendary king of the 7th century BC who was said to have added two months to the calendar, one being January which he named after Janus the God of 'beginnings'!!

Three prominent early Club members were Lord Middleton, Brigadier Gen. Sir Edward Spears (**later in the 1939/45 war Sir Winston Churchill's liaison officer with General de Gaulle**) and Sir John Squire, the poet and literary journalist.

Other prominent people attending Club dinners were:

Lord Lloyd

The Earl of Glasgow

Gen. Sir Hubert Gough (Commander of the Fifth Army on the Western Front in 1916/18)

Capt. (later Sir) Liddell Hart the military historian

C. B. Fry (the cricketer)

Mr. G. Ward Price

Lord Russell of Liverpool (one of the lawyers in the

team prosecuting Nazi war criminals)!

The Earl of Idlesleigh

Sir Charles Petrie (the historian)

Gen. Fuller (formerly chief staff officer of the Tank Corps in 1916/18 and author of a history of the Second World War was the subject of a special branch report marked 'secret')

Mr. Compton Mckenzie

Ian Hope Dundas (Mosley's chief of staff)

William Joyce (better known as 'Lord Haw Haw')

Mr. W.E.D. Allen (chairman of David Allen & Sons printers and publishers)

Mr. J. A. McNab

Lord Rothermere

Of the above, the three most prominent and active personalities behind the Blackshirt Movement and outwardly in support of Sir Oswald Mosley were ...

Lord Rothermere; Mr. W.E. Allen; Major Francis Yeats-Brown.

Amongst the very rich but lesser known members of the January Club and supporters of Sir Oswald Mosley was a Mr. A.C. Scrimgeour suspected of having given (in today's monetary terms) up to £250,000 to the Movement. Scrimgeour was known to be an admirer of the Fascist system and an anti-semitist. He lived at Honer Farm, Pagham, Bognor Regis, Sussex.

Sir Oswald Mosley was himself a very rich man. With the financial backing of such men as Scrimgeour, the 'Daily Mail' and the Italian Fascist Movement alleged to have given (in today's monetary terms) £1,000,000 and the donations alleged to be given by such huge industrial Companies as Imperial Chemical Industries, Courtaulds and the Coal Utilisation Council as well as two of the larger Brewery Companies the Blackshirt Movement was not lacking in funds.

Set alongside of the early history of the National Socialist Party in Germany when Hitler succeeded in convincing the leading Bankers and Industrialists that support of him would ensure their growth and prosperity there is an easily recognisable pattern of similarity, in the attempts to obtain the support of influential figures in all aspects and at all levels of Society.

It is perhaps permissable to raise an eyebrow when it is disclosed that Lord Russell of Liverpool later played a part as a lawyer in the British prosecuting team in the Nazi war crimes trials.

Which side was he working for when he went to the January Club dinners? Which side did he favour when he sat as a prosecuting counsel? Even Lord Shawcross admits to having some mixed thoughts when he lead the trials in the years after the war.

One of the most significant pointers to the efficiency and attention to detail which is to be found in 'The Black Book' is the absence of all the names listed from the 2820 quoted with the exception of one ... Brigadier General Sir Edward Spears is listed. Sir Edward, it was of course, who later in 1939/45 became Sir Winston Churchill's liaison officer with General de Gaulle! Either Sir Edward had changed his mind regarding where his allegiances should lie or he had throughout been working for Sir Winston Churchill. Put bluntly, he had joined to infiltrate, because Sir Winston would not otherwise have had access to that kind of information until he had become Prime Minister.

Under cover of the title of Home Correspondent for the 'Daily Mail' a gentleman, Mr. Ian Hope Dundas, was acting as liaison officer between the British and Italian Fascists.

An MI5 report had him listed as Sir Oswald Mosley's Chief of Staff.

William Joyce (known during the Second World War as Lord Haw Haw) who broadcasted from Germany proved, eventually, to be an uneasy bedfellow for Sir Oswald Mosley, and was disowned by the Movement.

The extent of pro-Nazi feelings amongst some of the most influential people in Britain is almost beyond belief of the reader today. There is no secret that the Prince of Wales (later King Edward VIII) was pro-Hitler, and had said so quite openly before his abdication.

It is a quixotic reflection that it was not because of his pro-Fascist feelings he was forced to abdicate but because of his affair with Mrs. Simpson! Yet another indication, surely, of the preoccupation of the Royal family and the Establishment with domestic squabbles and personalities when danger signs were flashing across the Channel from Germany for all to see.

Or ... was the affair with Mrs Simpson simply a convenient vehicle for the removal of a rebellious King with dangerous thoughts? King George VI's task was not an enviable one.

Of all his aides and advisors when he became King, King George VI's greatest confidant was Lord Halifax, labelled by some as 'the appeaser par excellence'.

It was Lord Halifax who had worked so industriously to recognise Mussolini's Italian sovereignty over Abyssinia and true or not it was Hitler's adjutant Fritz Wiedmann, who was alleged to have quoted Lord Halifax as saying 'I would like to see, as the culmination of my work, the Fuhrer entering London at the side of the English King amid the acclamation of the English people'. But would the English people have given their acclamation?

Lord Rothermere of the 'Daily Mail' had, over the years, veered between being rabidly anti-German to singing the praises of Hitler in 1939, having flirted from time to time with Mosley's Blackshirt Movement. It is generally considered this action was more out of pique with a Government which had failed to heed his earlier remonstrations in the 'Daily Mail' that the air force must be strengthened.

Lord Beaverbrook in the 'Daily Express' had at one time praised Hitler for his successful restoration of Germany. But both men, in their newspapers, as the inevitability of war became apparent and the real intentions of Hitler and his Third Reich became obvious, began their campaigns condemning Germany and the Nazis.

Only *'The Mirror'* had consistently condemned the feebleness of the Government which was reflected in the vain and gullible man who led it ... Neville Chamberlain, and had repeatedly warned about Germany.

Sir Oswald Mosley evidently believing in the ultimate victory of the Nazis and his own status in the new regime to be, made no effort to obtain Parliamentary representation convinced that Parliament, as such, would cease to exist.

This then was the situation amongst the ruling classes of Britain and the Civil and Military administration during the years before Winston Churchill became Prime Minister.

The apparently fortress like foundations of the British Empire were not so solid as they appeared to be.

This no doubt was encouraging to Hitler whose Intelligence sources would have alerted him to the truth. Hitler's desire for cooperation with England is expressed repeatedly in *'Mein Kampf'*. In the early pages we read "there was only one possible ally in Europe. That was England." And in the closing pages "For a long time to come there will be only two Powers in Europe with which it may be possible for Germany to conclude an alliance. These Powers are Great Britain and Italy".

Whilst Hitler was writing *'Mein Kampf'*, Italy had already become a Fascist State and was eventually to form the Axis with Germany.

That the British/Italian link was no dream is borne out by the support and acclamation given by Lord Halifax to Mussolini on his success in Abyssinia. Whilst being wrong about Great Britain, Hitler never the less was right about Italy, in that the country was ripe for a fascist anti-semitic conversion.

That there was a strong anti-semitic undercurrent flowing through British Society there was no doubt but it did not mean that the anti-semitic hysteria which Hitler had whipped up in the German people, and Mussolini in Italy, could be repeated in Britain.

In Britain a long hard battle had been fought in the previous century for the emancipation of the Catholics and the Jews in public life and it had been less than 80 years since a Bill had been passed permitting Jews into Parliament.

Soon after Winston Churchill's appointment as Prime Minister emergency legislation became necessary to stop the flood of anti-war and anti-semitic comments being expressed in Parliament and amongst prominent members of the Establishment.

Whatever people thought they were not allowed to say it.

One Tory M.P. was imprisoned. Needless to say Captain Archibald Maule Ramsey's name does not appear in 'The Black Book', whilst Lord Halifax and Mr. Chamberlain are listed.

The fact that such legislation became necessary is some measure of the strength of opinion existing. That this swell of opinion should be largely within the ruling and upper classes presents an interesting question as to 'Why'?

Sir Oswald Mosley had already been interned for the duration.

Was it 'big business' protecting Industry and Investments – some no doubt – in Germany? Or was it obsequious support by the Court of a Monarch who had Germanic origins?

One thing was certain ... such feelings were not shared by the Jewish population.

With such a scenario having been enacted in England in the years before the outbreak of war it is not, perhaps, so surprising to read of the alleged readiness of the Channel Island Authorities to cooperate with the Germans and to disclose 'wrongdoers'. Their legislature limiting the Jewish degree of participation in Island affairs had been established for centuries.

Each of the Channel Islands was a small community, defenceless, and imprisoned on an island with no means of escape. When the occupying forces arrived notices appeared immediately warning the population that an assault on a

German, whether Civil or Military would be responded to by execution to the quota of 20 to 1.

For lesser crimes imprisonment or deportation to a European Concentration Camp would be the punishment.

Such sentences are described by the two eye-witness contributors to this book.

The Islanders were of course not aware but in Warsaw, following the collapse of Polish resistance a German soldier was killed by a Pole in a fight over a girl. When the police arrived the pub was empty. As a reprisal the Wehrmacht stopped trams, forced people to dismount and shot 50.

It happened to be the reprisal quota in Poland!

Alex von dem Busche, a Germany Army Officer who had planned to assassinate Hitler remarked: 'I watched. I could not believe it'.

Anyone, before or during the war, or to this day who still believes that the Germans would have behaved any differently once Britain had been occupied is living in a world of fantasy.

Before the invasion of Poland it is recorded that Hitler, when talking to army generals said: "Close your hearts to pity. Act brutally. Eighty million people must obtain what is their right".

And, in the years before the war, it is alleged, when talking to Herman Rauschning, Hitler said ...

"We must be prepared for the hardest struggle that a nation has ever had to face. Only through this test of endurance can we become ripe for the domination to which we are called. It will be my duty to carry on this war regardless of losses.

The sacrifice of lives will be immense. We all of us know what World War means. As a people we shall be forged to the hardness of steel. All that is weak will fall away from us. But the forged central block will last for ever. I have no fear of annihilation. We shall have to abandon much that is dear to us and today seems irreplaceable. Cities will become heaps of ruins, noble monuments of architecture will disappear forever. This time our sacred soil will not be spared. But I am not afraid of this".

Perhaps Hitler had once heard quoted the lines from the Song of the Curassiers in Schiller's 'Wallenstein' ...

> *Und setzet ihr nicht das Leben ein*
> *Nie wird euch das Leban gewonnen sein.*
> *(And if you do not stake your life*
> *You will never win life for yourself)*

In the German language there is a word for which there is no English equivalent. **Weltanschauung** literally means 'Outlook on the World'. In general German use this means a whole system of associated ideas together in an organic unity – ideas of human life, human values, cultural and religious ideas, politics, economics, in fact a totalitarian view of human existence. This Hitler succeeded in translating in real terms into the Nazi declaration of faith and national pride. He propounds these ideas in *'Mein Kampf'*, and presented them to a pride starved nation in the form of National Socialism.

No apology is made for this deviation into German History for had the politicians, the philosophers, the historians and the thinkers of other nations paid more attention to events in Germany in the decade before the war, there might have been no war, and no Holocaust. With no Holocaust there would have been no gaschambers.

Wilhelm Mohnke

Accused of slaughtering British P.O.W.s

Nazi Veterans

During the Post War Nuremberg war crimes trials the SS was declared a criminal organisation. Allied Judges declared all members of the SS had knowingly participated in crimes against humanity.

The Chairman of the OdR bearers association, Wolfram Kertz (78) of Lohmar, near Bonn, when questioned denied there was any connection with the SS and OdR. He later admitted that there were at least 50, perhaps more SS members in the association. Fritz Derges had been Hitler's adjutant and is now treasurer of the association's benevolant fund. But Kertz denied it was the notorious Colonel Fritz Derges. Kertz admitted that Derges did in fact come from Celle and had been an Obersturmbannfuehrer (Lt. Col.) in the SS Viking Panzer Division. Regarding Wilhelm Mohnke when pressed Kertz admitted General Mohnke was an OdR Ritterkreuz member.

Note of interest: The design of the ties worn by the Nazi veterans of the association will make a swastika, by cutting the zig-zag white line in two places, and placing one upon the other. Typical of the British

attitude towards German atrocity subjects was British Ambassador Sir Nigel Broomfield's refusal to discuss the matter.

Flashback to 1936—Sir Oswald Mosley returning the salute of Fascist Blackshirts during a rally in the East End of London.

Chrzanowski:
Denies war atrocities

Andre Bakunowicz:
Suspect

Szymon Serafinowicz:
On bail

*Will these men
be brought to trial?*

it was just after the hearse had received from respects
so I went with my cart to get it but, coming up the hill
to Hauteville via Bordage the wheels gave way & there I was
I dare not leave it for help. eventually a child went &
told Mr Hewlett & him & 2 or 3 of his friends came to help
of course we were wet & frozen. What a life! so of course as
you can imagine every thing was practically at a standstill
the italian & russian prisoners of war were made to cut
trees down & saw into logs, for the germans it was happening in front of us for the still high & mighty. many of the
germans would have surrended but the highest boss of
them would not do so, in fact some tried to kill him but
it was them who got killed. no more clubs, nothing the germans
told us if the English landed we would be taken as quickly
& no locking of doors, of course we took no notice but as
we were told the new concrete blocks on White Rock were
for gas chambers we were afraid we would never be saved.
So in the end I managed to get to Richards by fairs I
know not how. I told them we thought the war was finishing
they knew nothing or dare not say. anyway I had a
little of something to eat. Sometime during all this
_____ mr Hewletts friend a Blackmarketer would
help _____ to get her fish supplies & sometimes, crab
in with an old pram & smuggled to her house some of it at
great risk for her to Black market, it was shocking what she
got in food & money. mr Hewlett did her accounts for her
she would say you are always well up with the money
never at a loss & she said, Well if people were taking &
gave you 2/6 you gave them change for 2/- or if some one gave
you & you gave change for 10/- if they complained which
wasnt very often & they were too busy after their fish
you pretended it was a mistake, she must have been well
off after the war but, her husband soon died & after about

A page from the wartime recollections of Mrs Betty Corkett

GASCHAMBERS

Reproduced opposite is a page from a book of wartime recollections written by Mrs Betty Corkett for her daughter Ann. Mrs Corkett lived in Guernsey throughout the occupation. The underlined words are "the Germans told us if the British landed we would be taken and used as shields, and no locking of doors. Of course we took no notice but, as we were told the new concrete blocks on White Rock were for gaschambers, we were afraid we would never be saved".

Beryl S. Ozanne was a nurse in Guernsey hospital throughout the occupation and on page 56 of her book "*A Peep Behind the Screens*" there is further reference to gaschambers. "I had to pass along the road where the Germans were building their underground tunnels. When we saw all the work going on there, once again rumour was rife. There was talk of gaschambers" ... "Knowing even the troops were getting short of food, were they that desperate? Did they intend reducing the population?"

On page 57 the extent of the Nazi 'net' can be judged from Beryl Ozanne's description of forced labour ... "The labour force used to build bunkers, gun emplacements and other defences" ... consisted of ... "men from many different countries; French, Spaniards, Japanese, African, Chinese, Poles, Rumanians" ... "Some could hardly stand but were made to work until they dropped and had to be carried back to their camp by fellow prisoners"

Betty Corkett and Beryl Ozanne were of course not alone in hearing about the gaschambers. Mrs Brockley in her testimony in this book (see page161) has her opinions and the other contributor Vassili Marempolski, (who worked as a Ukrainian prisoner in the Jersey tunnels and met a Russian

111

Jew who had been a prisoner in Auschwitz), also believed the tunnels were intended as gaschambers; whilst Tommy Syms during the last year of his imprisonment in Biberach (see page 199) tells of hearing his elders discussing fearfully the possibility they may all be gassed when hundreds of American Jews arrived in the camp.

It would now seem that by 1942 the extermination of large numbers of people throughout occupied Europe, including the Channel Islands, had become common knowledge. (See page 22 for Emmi Bonhöffer's story). The stories of gassings and shootings, in the miraculous way in which news, for thousands of years, has filtered through by word of mouth at grassroots level, could not be denied.

Despite the denials by Government and Military officials then and since, that they had no knowledge of what was going on, such denials are rebutted by the historical records of military discussion as to whether or not Auschwitz should be bombed.

Inmates of that dreadful place, afterwards gave evidence that they had prayed they **would** be bombed by the Allied planes which flew overhead, but they were not.

Auschwitz was not the only camp designated by Himmler for the extermination of Jews, and well before the decision to turn Birkenau into a killing machine other camps, where gassing was carried out indiscriminately, had been established at Belzec, Treblinka, Sobibor and Chelkno, thus emphasising the desire of the Nazis to retain the covert nature of the operation.

Gassing by carbon monoxide was the method used at the time, but the problem, as had been revealed earlier during the mass shootings of whole populations of villages and towns of men, women and children, after being driven from where they lived to places just outside for execution, was the disposal of the bodies.

Shooting, where large numbers of people were involved, was a long, messy and unpleasant method even for those perpetrating the deeds, but the disposal of the bodies remained the greater problem.

It was obvious to Himmler who was in charge of this operation that a simpler, quicker, more efficient method had to be found and gassing, as we have seen, was undoubtedly the answer, coupled with the incineration of the bodies.

In addition to Auschwitz/Birkenau and the four camps already mentioned other camps had developed the system.

Ruth Foster, a German Jewess, sought out in a remote German village, was sent to Latvia, and from there to Stutthof concentration camp near Gdansk in Poland ... she says "The first thing we noticed (as we approached) was a strange and powerful smell, like hard-boiled eggs that had boiled dry. We soon found out this was the combined smell of the gaschamber and crematorium". She was the only member of her family to survive.

An Auschwitz inmate tells of a visit by Himmler in 1942 to inspect the problem which had arisen in Birkenau where corpses, considered buried (this was before the incinerators had been built) had, with the arrival of spring and the thawing of the ground, come to the surface of the boggy terrain. He describes watching other inmates in the most appalling conditions digging out the corpses, carrying them to mass graves and pouring inflammable liquid over the heap of bodies and setting it alight. No doubt the first practical acceptance that burning was the only solution.

This took weeks, and when the work was completed the men who had survived were taken away and also killed.

Himmler, probably with memories of 'Kristelnacht' and the difficulties created by the shooting of 20,000 Jews outside Riga, still in his mind, realised that a better solution had to be found.

One incident after another in the years leading up to and during the early years of the war had made it clear that the fewer witnesses there were of these killings, the better.

It is well to remember this when the case for the Channel Islands as a permanent site for an extermination centre is argued later in this book.

With the combined conditions of starvation, dysentery, cholera and typhus, the death rate from these diseases was almost as high as the systematic killings, and exposed the guards and officials controlling the camps to a similar danger.

In dry weather a pall of dust hung over many of the camps, and dust is of course a carrier of deadly typhus.

With the advance of the Nazis into Russia, Hungary and other countries, the sad stream of dejected, cowed people increased. The trainloads of people packed tight into cattle trucks without food, water, sanitation and wearing in most cases only the clothing they had been wearing when arrested, rumbled slowly across hundreds of miles. On arrival at Auschwitz or one of the other camps, the trucks, when the doors were flung open, would be found to contain only the dead. In winter such occasions were more common, (see Tommy Syms testimony, page 197).

Winters in Poland, Russia and Eastern Germany could be particularly severe and there is documentary evidence that the building of the gaschambers and incinerators in Auschwitz/Birkenau was frequently held up because of delays in the supply of building materials caused by the weather.

It is important to note this when considering the case for a centralised extermination camp, such as the Channel Islands.

With the cessation of hostilities following the capitulation or defeat of Britain there would have been no danger to shipping from (enemy/British) aircraft or navy, to ships taking Jews from England to the Channel Islands, and no hold-ups from bad weather.

The evolution of Auschwitz from, in early days, a comparatively small concentration camp to a huge camp devoted entirely to the mass extermination of people, was almost accidental.

With the German invasion of Poland and the need for a convenient place to send the Jews from the Polish ghettos, Auschwitz was chosen. From here those able to work were deported to places throughout Germany to work. As the numbers increased so did the need for a larger camp retaining both Jews and Russian prisoners so it became a Work/ Concentration Camp. With the conditions in which they were living came death from disease. With the higher death rate cremation was the only solution and so the first experiments in Auschwitz and later in the Birkenau cottages began.

By the middle of 1941 it was apparent the experiments being carried out in the small rooms or cellars were going to be inadequate. So, simultaneously with the development in methods of gassing, plans were ordered to be drawn up for a better method of cremation.

Birkenau was a huge new camp ordered by Himmler to be built within three kilometres of Auschwitz. This camp finally contained 125,000 inmates, largely Jews, Poles and some Russian prisoners and these would be used to build the gaschambers and crematoria in Birkenau.

The working prisoners were crammed into barrack rooms in which they were forced to live and sleep in two and three tier wooden bunks measuring approximately 3' high by 3' wide ... (see Fig. 51 Guernsey 1944 page 143)

The plans for Birkenau camp were changed a number of times as the size and the needs of the place became more evident. In its completed state it was about one third the size of Alderney. The conditions were horrific and it is only those who lived through that hell who could make a judgement as to whether the stories of cannibalization were true or **not**. **Were** they only the imaginings of a fevered brain?

Experiments with an alternative gassing agent to Carbon Monoxide began in late 1942, in the converted Morgue of the Auschwitz crematorium.

Into this gaschamber people were bundled tightly without room to sit down or fall down and a gasproof door was slammed upon them. Through an aperture in the roof or wall, pesticide pellets were dropped into the room. The heat from the close packed bodies created a deadly gas called Zyclon B.

The aperture was closed.

It took them two days to die.

Because the killing, the smell and the cries of the dying could not be kept secret from the inhabitants of Auschwitz the experiments were stopped and transferred to two cottages, near the Birkenau camp, which had been converted for the purpose.

Here again, the Nazi awareness of the need for secrecy is apparent.

Prisoners in Auschwitz, still with the strength to work, were required to remove the bodies under conditions which were unspeakable. Clambering upon one another for air the dying became entangled. Fear and the loss of control of bodily functions as death took over, created conditions almost beyond imagination.

In the process of building the barracks a basic crematorium had been built but with the influx of people it became evident a much larger more efficient method was required.

These decisions were arrived at around the beginning of January 1942, around the same time that the excavation of the tunnels in the Channel Islands began.

Having established by trial and error a satisfactory method of mass, swift extermination, the means had now to be provided.

There already existed under Himmler's authority an architect's department, the SS Zentralbauleinung, in Berlin. A similar office was set up in Auschwitz staffed by top architects, designers and engineers.

The express task of this high ranking group was to cooperate with the German engineering company Topf & Sons who were already manufacturing crematoria for concentration camps.

The discussions resulted in Kurt Prüfer, the chief designer at Topf & Sons, producing an oven which could burn two bodies simultaneously. To contain the ovens the architects designed a simple but strong and efficient structure with 50' chimneys. The building would contain as many as four groups of two tier ovens. But no sooner had they been built than they proved inadequate for the demand.

It seems also, that no sooner was one problem overcome than another arose. Earlier in the stages of experimentation the compressing of very large numbers of people into large areas presented difficulties. When the bodies came to be removed it was found that people in their dying throes struggled, fought, panicked and became entangled with one another.

The scene must have been reminiscent of Holbein's 'Dance of Death or Michelangelo's 'Judgement', equalled only perhaps by Bernstein's film of German prisoners removing the thousands of dead found lying around Belsen and Auschwitz, when the Allied troops arrived.

In the earlier stages of Auschwitz development the conveying of bodies from the gassing area to the incinerators took time, so the provision of a building which would incorporate both functions became the ultimate objective of the designers.

Finally, after having passed through various stages of amendments a design for a subterranean construction consisting of five sets of three-oven incinerators combined with gassing facilities was agreed and work began.

This is an appropriate moment to pause and compare the similarities in layout of these constructions with the plans and photographs of the so called 'underground hospitals' in Jersey and Guernsey.

The siting of the 'extermination factories' had become a matter of some argument between the Top Brass in Berlin and Himmler.

Himmler wanted to get on with the job of extermination, and to that purpose required certain types to work for him from the camps. Goering had other ideas and wanted priority in the use of the camp inmates for his own projects.

Finally, it was decided that four 'factories' should be built near the Birkenau camp the first being Crematorium 2.

One of the refinements incorporated into Crematorium 2 was a track for conveying trolleys loaded with corpses for the incinerators. Other innovations were incorporated such as a ventilation system for the rapid extraction of the poison gas (to permit the entry for the extraction of the bodies), gas detectors, gas tight doors and a plentiful supply of water and electricity, the latter required for the ovens of course, and the water for the washing down process.

From the early days when Auschwitz had been chosen for the systematic murder of Jews, electricity was a necessity.

The internationally famous Company IG Farben (now better known as AEG) had been invited to set up in Auschwitz a generating station which was to be staffed from the cheap labour available in the camp, so electricity, from the outset was no problem.

It is perhaps appropriate to pause here and ponder on the wisdom of those inmates of Auschwitz who prayed that the Allies should bomb the camp. Had the generating station been destroyed the incineration process would have come to a halt and many thousands of lives might have been saved.

Was there, even then, an element of influence within the Allied (British in particular) War Directive which demanded that a great company such as IG Farben in which 'The City' undoubtedly had a share, should be left intact?

To return to similarities in design, by referring to the diagram on page 139 of Crematorium 2 there is provision for a chute and a staircase (bottom left hand corner) the purpose of the chute was for sliding corpses down into the basement. This was before the design included both gaschambers and incinerators at the same level.

In a later blue-print the chute has been dispensed with, the stairs remaining. (See page 119).

Steps leading to Gaschambers

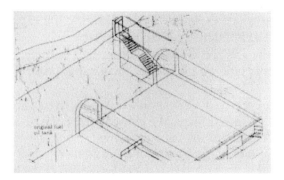

Those for extermination were walked down the steps into the subterranean chambers, where they were gassed and burned.

With the completion of all four of the Crematoria it has been estimated that the daily incineration capacity in Auschwitz could have reached 4756 persons.

There is some doubt about this for almost certainly there would have been stoppages when the 'cleaning up' process was required and there is also the possibility of mechanical breakdowns.

The Crematoria were built as close to the railway line as possible to facilitate the unloading, when required, of prisoners directly into the Crematoria for gassing otherwise they were walked to a nearby barrack room.

There was also the possibility of trains arriving with most of the people on board already dead, and this too would have held up the transferral process.

The slowest part of the operation always had been, and remained, the removal of the corpses from the gassing rooms to the incinerators. This still had to be a manual operation, admittedly made easier by the introduction of tracked trolleys.

How the designers arrived at what they considered to be the suitable size for the gassing chambers remains unsolved, but the previous experience gained during the experimental period was undoubtedly used as a guide.

Whereas the incineration process had become a science and output could be calculated, the gassing process was less accurate.

Each of the four Crematoria was a different size with a different 'disposal' capacity consequently the sizes of the gassing 'chambers' or cubicles varied. But the larger the number of bodies the greater the heat generated, and it was upon the heat generated that the effectiveness of the hydrogen cyanide pellets named Zyclon B depended.

A modern crematorium oven can turn an average sized body into ashes in approximately 1½ hours and a further hour is required before the ashes are cool enough to be retrieved and stored.

It may be assumed that most of the bodies incinerated in Auschwitz were of medium to small size.

Two of the crematoria each contained 15 ovens and the two other crematoria each contained 8 ovens making a total of 46 ovens accepting 3 corpses at a time, thus achieving a total intake at any one time of 138 bodies.

As the ovens were not allowed to cool down, the time required for incineration might have been considerably reduced but it is unlikely that the disposal rate would have averaged more than 2000 to 2500 in a 20 hour day, although it has been suggested it was twice that number.

Against these estimations must be set the time required for gassing, and, as has already been said, this could take up to 48 hours.

The area required for such a number of people, **very** tightly packed, would be about half the size of a football pitch, or a total of some 32 rooms each 12' x 10', would contain approximately 4750 people.

Now examine the measurements of the 'underground hospital' area or shelter in Guernsey. These are ... (See page 145).

Central Rooms   100' in length x
                       16' in width x
                       11½' in height

Hospital   65' in length'
                       15' in width x
                       11' in height

The corridors are 8½ wide and 11' in height

Including the Cinema, Mortuary, Store Room, Wards, Guard Room and Dispensary there are 11 'chambers' each measuring approximately 1000 sq feet.

If the rate of disposal estimated for the Auschwitz/ Birkenau Crematoria was correct at 4750 then 5 chambers would be required for one day's supply of bodies.

As there were only approximately 10 or 11 chambers this amounts to two days supply of bodies bearing in mind each group of people would take two days to die.

The calculations shown are for the 'hospital' wards, the Central Room chambers being somewhat larger would have taken even more people in a similar number of chambers.

It is however unlikely that these chambers would have been used for gassing purposes. Much more likely the classified possessions of the prisoners such as hair, shoes, spectacles, suitcases, would have been stored in an orderly fashion in much the same way as they were found by General Vasilly Yakovlevich Petrenko of the Soviet Army on entering Auschwitz.

A careful examination of the plan for Hohlgangsanlage 40 in Guernsey (see page 145) will indicate the positions of the escape shafts down which would have been dropped the cyanide pellets. In the top left section will be seen the position of the well, from which water would have been drawn for the washing down process required after each gassing. All passages and rooms slope towards the La Vassalerie entrance, to which would have been fitted a gasproof door or Air Lock.

It will be noted that La Vassalerie gives access to Ho 40 and that only one passage way provides access from Ho 40 to the larger complex referred to as a 'Shelter' or 'Munition Store' the main access being via the main Entrance. This complex is referred to as Ho 7. There is an unfinished tunnel, middle centre, with an unfinished Escape Shaft No. 3.

One significant difference between the Guernsey and Jersey tunnelling used as hospitals is the absence of steps in the Guernsey complex, into the subterranean area, as were provided in the Auschwitz construction.

The reason for this is the ease of access to the tunnelling by passageways dug into the hillside. The victims would have been marched straight in and the doors sealed. All that was required were the 'escape shafts' or chutes down which the pellets would have been dropped.

In the case of Jersey the stairs were provided (Ltr R) and a chute. There is also an unfinished escape shaft or chute at the end of the passage (Ltr G) and two Air Locks or Gas Proof Doors are fitted at the end of the two entrances from Cap Verd and Meadowbank. (Letter C).

In Ho 8 on Jersey, as they exist today, only eight 'wards' are in use but had the excavations continued a similar number of 'wards' or chambers would have been available, as in Guernsey.

The 'wards' have drainage channels and narrow gauge railway lines are still to be seen and, as with the Guernsey construction, floors slope towards an entrance, yet further proof of the recognition that a 'washing down' process would have been essential.

These are the facts illustrating the similarities between the Channel Island tunnelling and the plans discovered by the Soviet Army in Berlin in 1945, taken to Moscow and stored in their World War II archives until 1991, when access was permitted to the 'Special Trophies Archive'.

Hearing of this, Historian Professor Gerald Fleming asked permission to visit the archives. In order to establish the maximum degree of professionalism in the investigation and research the help of Robert Jan Van Pelt a Professor of Architecture from Holland was engaged. It is on their collective premise the conclusions set out in this book are based.

In order that the reader may arrive at a fair, unbiased judgement it is important that the **'scenario of possibility'** that Britain had capitulated or been beaten, must be accepted.

The reader should also accept the fact, generally acknowledged by all historians, writers, journalists and politicians, that **had** Britain come beneath the Nazi jackboot the 'Final Solution' would very quickly have been applied to the 450,000 Jews in Britain, and that some means of disposal would have to be found.

Setting aside the logical arguments and the psychological background the similarities in design and practical detail between the Birkenau Crematoriums and the Channel Islands tunnels are impressive.

(a) The tunnels and the Crematoria were all fitted with gas proof doors.

(b) Escape shafts of similar size existed in both Auschwitz and the Channel Islands. (They were used in Birkenau for inserting the hydrogen cyanide pellets)

(c) Chutes were incorporated into the design of the Auschwitz/Birkenau gaschambers. A chute still exists in the Jersey 'underground hospital'.

(d) A 'ventilation' system was installed in the gassing areas of Auschwitz/Birkenau. A ventilation system exists in the Jersey tunnelling.

(e) Artificial reservoirs were built within the Channel Islands 'underground hospitals'. A good water supply was used and was available at the Auschwitz/Birkenau camps.

(f) Electricity is an important factor in the operation of the 'killing machine'. It was freely available both in Auschwitz and in the Channel Islands.

(g) Staircases are provided in the Auschwitz Crematoria and also in the Jersey and Guernsey 'underground hospitals'.

(h) Narrow gauge rail tracking was installed in Auschwitz/ Birkenau for transportation of bodies. Similar track was installed, and can still be seen, in the Jersey tunnelling.

(j) On Sept 18th 1942 two Heilman & Littman steam engines arrived to power the compressors for the excavation machinery required for the tunnelling and by November a wooden structure was being built in preparation for the construction of a 50' chimney. The design and measurements of this chimney were identical to those built in Birkenau for the new Crematoria.

Taking into account the number and size of the chambers in both Islands, the mass murder of Britain's half million Jews and anti-Nazis would have been accomplished in less than a year.

But what would have been the alternative to using the Channel Islands for the purpose?

Would the Nazis have waited until they had obtained full control of the country before beginning to build the Crematoria? And where would they have built them?

Not in England, perhaps in Wales, but more likely in Scotland. But could this have been carried out discreetly bearing in mind the rumours already circulating throughout Europe about the gassings?

Some students of the subject argue that the transportation of hundreds of thousands of people from one end of England to the other would have been equally suspect, but the following figures should be noted.

In 1938 there were 234,000 Jews in London, 38,000 in Manchester and a lesser number in Leeds, the remainder being spread around the Country. This figure increased considerably just before the outbreak of war and at the outbreak of war the Jewish population of Britain has been estimated at 450,000 including the unregistered and registered.

Mr Michael Whine, Chief Executive of the Board of Deputies of British Jews, Dr David Cesarani of the Wiener Library and Mr Ben Belfgott, Chairman of Yad Vashem (the Museum of the Holocaust in Jerusalem) are all agreed that this is a fair estimate. They are also agreed that, had the Nazis won the war, the Jews in Britain would have been exterminated, with a probable further 50,000 British.

But this is where their agreement with the Author's hypothesis ends.

The general assumption with most Historians is that there were only two alternatives open to the Nazis for the disposal of the half million ... transportation to Auschwitz or the establishment of an extermination camp in Britain.

Transporting half a million people across the Channel and through France to Auschwitz seems an easy solution **but** it should be born in mind that Hitler did not want to offend the collaborating British hierarchy and almost certainly, news would eventually have filtered through from France.

Vichy France had had no compunction in collaborating with the Nazis in setting up the Drancy Concentration Camp in the centre of Paris from which tens of thousands of Jews were despatched to Auschwitz, and other extermination camps, so it is from such sources news would have come to Britain.

In the transportation of such large numbers there was the problem of possible train breakdowns, the long journey involved and a period of year when weather would bring the operation to a halt, necessitating the setting up in Britain of concentration camps to hold the victims pending transportation.

Frequently raised is the question 'why, if the Nazis had reached the stage of designing a perfect 'killing machine' should they need another in the Channel Islands?'

Dr David Cesarani, Director of the Institute of Contemporary History and the Wiener Library Ltd., a very respected historian on the subject argues that the Germans did not carry out killings locally and that the **underground gaschambers** (the emphasis is the Author's) at Auschwitz/ Birkenau were not built for gassing purposes originally, but were adapted from mortuaries. (See Israel Gutman et al (eds) Anatomy of the Auschwitz Death Camp 1994).

This of course is perfectly true, as has already been outlined, but this hypothesis ignores the evidence of the evolution of the place as a work camp (as it was originally intended by the Nazis) from an expedience, which is what the original Auschwitz mortuaries were, into the finished product.

Local killings were of course carried out throughout the occupied countries and it was in fact the problems arising from this method which led to the demand for a scientific solution, and eventually to the Crematoria built in Birkenau.

The problem of 'disposal' was being met by all the camps.

Dr David Cesarani points to the transportation of Jews from Rhodes and Corfu to Auschwitz as some indication that the Auschwitz/Birkenau establishment would have served all purposes and needs.

But would it?

At the time of the German occupation of Greece the Channel Island tunnels excavation had only just commenced. There was no where else to send Jews but to Auschwitz. Had not the Nazi occupation forces in the Channel Islands sent the Jews there to Auschwitz also?

It is an interesting observation on the determination of the Nazis to reach into every corner of the occupied countries in their search for Jews that they should have scoured Rhodes, an island with a population no greater than that of Jersey, for the few dozen Jews who happened to be there.

If the 'Final Solution' was extended to an Island 14 miles from Turkey, then the fate of the 450,000 Jews in Britain could only be a foregone conclusion!

It has been suggested that Dr Cruickshank, the author of the Official History of the Occupation, expressed the thought that it would not have been necessary to create gaschambers in the Islands for the disposal of a mere 100,000 for these could have been sent to Auschwitz. What a narrow parochial view! Yet a view reflected in book after book about the Nazi Occupation of the Islands, with the exception of those written by Peter King and Madeline Bunting.

Surely, if the general situation had reached a point where the disposal of the Channel Islanders (as stated in Baron Von Aufsess' diary) was under discussion then a similar situation would be imminent for the Jewish population in Britain?

As we have already seen, and can see through the information in 'The Black Book', whilst transportation and disposal systems might temporarily collapse, the arrest of Jews and anti-Fascists proceeded apace. Collection points were needed, and as remarked elsewhere, by 1945 there were 5000 of these throughout occupied Europe, eventually, with Teutonic thoroughness they would have been emptied, but to where? And how? (See page 111 Beryl Ozanne's list of nationalities who were slave workers in Guernsey).

The extermination of large numbers in Britain would have demanded the very rapid establishment of a large Crematorium with attendant concentration camps.

Scotland, as we have already seen, would seem to be the countryside most suitable for such an establishment, and the most discreet. But there would have been the difficulty of gathering in and moving some 300,000 (approximate figures) people out of London and a further 100,000 from Manchester.

But there **was** an alternative. The Channel Islands.

It might be argued that the removal of half a million people to the Channel Islands presented greater difficulties than the two other alternatives ... but not so.

London and Manchester are large Ports (or were at that time) where ships could be loaded with human cargo and despatched with the utmost secrecy and discretion. It is easier to load people on to ships than into cattle trucks, as the slave traders learned a few hundred years ago.

The collection and movement of people to the Docks would have been geared to the shipping capacity available at any one time.

Had Hitler invaded immediately after Dunkirk there would admittedly, have been no underground tunnels, but by the end of 1942 (when he should have completed his defeat of Soviet Russia) work was already in full swing on the tunnels in the Channel Islands.

The occupation of the Channel Islands had begun only 34 days after Dunkirk. Ten months later, one month before he invaded the Soviet Union, Hitler issued his directive that massive fortification works must commence immediately. At that time he was obviously so confident of a successful conclusion to his invasion of the USSR and Britain's capitulation he was prepared to spend more time, and labour, on building fortifications and tunnels in the Channel Islands than he was on reinforcing the defences along the coastline from Dieppe to Cherbourg.

What was in Hitler's mind when he issued such a directive?

Much of the work on the tunnels, which was at its height during 1942 and tailed off in 1943, was completed, although due to the effect of D-Day, many tunnels were left unfinished.

What we are studying here is **not** the conditions and the situation which prevailed during the war but the conditions and the situation which would have existed had we lost.

The tunnels could have been completed in less than two years. In the mean time, Alderney, evacuated of civilians before the Occupation, would have immediately become a concentration camp housing British prisoners pending the completion of the gaschambers in Jersey and Guernsey.

Following the usual pattern the importation of prisoners from Europe would not have been necessary as British Jews and others would have been used.

We have seen that Birkenau, holding 125,000 inmates was only one third the size of Alderney, there would therefore have been plenty of room, eventually, for one hundred thousand prisoners awaiting execution.

As with most concentration camps during the war, large numbers, due to the conditions in which they would have been forced to live, would have died of typhus, cholera, dysentery and starvation.

Of the two possible scenarios in which Britain is defeated, the first, immediately after Dunkirk, the second after victory over the Soviet Union, the second would have found the tunnels in Jersey and Guernsey completed and ready for use.

We have traced the slow development, the evolution, by trial and error, of the machinery of mass extermination of human beings from gassing lorries and converted farmhouses to purpose built factories.

The mass extermination of 'unwanted' people as epitomised in the mentality and behaviour of the Nazis was similar to that of a murderer, or serial killer. Once having committed murder, once having killed, once having tasted of that drug, the second time becomes easier and the third easier still until the act ceases to have meaning except the urge to feed the need to kill.

The 'Final Solution' had become an unstoppable force carried along on its own momentum, and it would almost certainly have continued into an indefinite future, for **the very concept of 'The Master Race' tolerated no other interpretation.**

Evidence, from many parts of the world as recent as 1945, confirms that such a concept is as cogent today as ever it was.

In the Channel Islands there would have been a permanent, heavily defended, unassailable spot devoted solely to the elimination of unwanted people, for whatever reason, where every conceivable kind of atrocity could have been carried out away from prying eyes.

The clean winds which blow across the Channel Islands would have swept away the stench of burning flesh from the Crematoria.

No doubt in time, as generation had succeeded generation, the knowledge of the Channel Islands and its evil use would, except for the privileged few, have been ignored, forgotten, in much the same way as the German population turned their backs upon the atrocities being committed in the years up to the war. It is probable the majority of the British population of today could not name those institutions devoted solely to the care of the mentally sick nor do they know how the inmates of those places are being treated ... and dare it be stated? ... do they care?

These arguments are not fantasies but the realities of speculation and 'the might have been'.

The willingness to accept that previously nurtured concepts, probably held for a life time, are wrong, is a difficult, and for some impossible path to tread.

For some, such as politicians, writers, historians, teachers, the admission to oneself, let alone to the public, of misconception amounts to a confession of failing in the ability to think deeply enough.

But more mundane reasons for remaining obdurate are likely. There is loss of pride, of self respect, of position in society and perhaps a job, and equally devastating, the realisation of having given many years of one's life to a service or cause which proves to have feet of clay.

It is not surprising therefore that when faced with the unpalatable truth, flat denials are the only response.

The unpalatable truth for Britain is that, had we been subjected to similar trials and tribulations as other European nations and the Channel Islanders, we might well have behaved similarly, and it is for this reason successive British Governments have been reluctant to pursue any enquiries which might lead to disclosures proving we were, and are, little different from anyone else.

The Channel Islanders, if the myth of the 'underground hospitals' is exploded, may lose more than one million pounds of tourist revenue each year.

Are they likely to change their story?

For some, the idea of a Channel Islands adapted for the sole purpose of the extermination of people is so bizarre it is beyond belief and attracts the epithet of 'sensationalism'.

Yet ... before it happened ... who would have accepted that the industrialised extermination of a whole race would be contemplated, yet alone attempted, and yet more horrific, would have been carried out, had the Nazis been victorious?

It was as unbelievable before it happened as it was to suggest in 1940 that 30 years later Man would walk on the Moon.

But that is providing an excuse, for the message had been there for all to see who had access to Hitler's 'Mein Kampf'. It is not to be expected that many members of the general public would have read 'Mein Kampf' but as a declaration of national policy it should have been read by those who governed.

So, uncomfortable as it may be for the Channel Islanders and all those who have rejected the idea for whatever reason, there is more circumstantial evidence and supporting proof that the tunnels in the Channel Islands of Jersey and Guernsey would have become gaschambers for the ethnic cleansing policy of the Nazis, than there is that they were to be used as 'underground hospitals'.

In 1994, in preparation for the liberation celebrations of the Channel Islands and for VE day, a leaflet was issued by The German Military Underground Hospital in Guernsey.

The honesty of this leaflet is quite remarkable ... here is a quote ...

"Actually the Hospital was only in use for about six weeks, and it would not have been used then had not several hundreds of German wounded been brought over from France soon after D-Day. Their stay in this huge vault was scarcely beneficial, for after three or four weeks their faces were as white as sheets!".

"After six weeks' stay underground these sunshine starved patients were removed to surface hospitals"

"When the Germans moved the patients they took most of the hospital equipment with them. Unfortunately much more was removed by the British in 1945, hence the somewhat bare appearance of the hospital today".

Whilst the Guernsey Authorities in charge of the 'hospital' have been remarkably honest in their commentary indicating that the tunnels were never intended as hospitals but simply served as an emergency exigency, the Jersey Authorities, who incidentally, were the first of the two Islands to present them to the public as 'underground hospitals', have been careful over the years to foster the idea by an elaborate, almost theatrical, development to make the idea of 'hospital' more convincing.

Undoubtedly, as a commercial undertaking for the purpose of attracting tourists it has a lot to recommend it, and those responsible are to be congratulated for their foresight.

Unfortunately, the tenacity with which this story has been maintained has only served to warp the truth and to compound the history of the Occupation.

It has also helped to divert attention away from those aspects of the Occupation which both Island Authorities and the British prefer to leave unmentioned, for ... as we have seen ... one disclosure leads to another and one question leads to another.

There is an axiom which says 'if you say anything, however untrue, for long enough and loud enough, you can convince anyone of anything'.

This is undoubtedly true of the tunnels in the Channel Islands which have, for some 45 years now, been presented to the public as 'underground hospitals'.

Once said, supported as in Jersey, by all the paraphernalia of equipment, lighting, videos, sound effects, photographs etc., only the most inquisitive and enquiring minds would question the authenticity of the 'statements' as presented.

It is to the credit of Mr Michael Ginns, Secretary of the Channel Islands Occupation Society (Jersey) in producing the excellent book *'German Tunnels in the Channel Islands'* that he has made no attempt to hoodwink the public into believing the tunnels were intended as hospitals.

On page 6 of that book we find this statement ...

"Never are the functions of the tunnels mentioned and never is the word 'hospital' mentioned in connection with Ho 8 (an identification number used by the Nazis for the tunnels).

In August 1941 Professor Klüpfel, a Wehrmacht Geologist, visited Jersey, his diary can be inspected at the British Museum. The above words are an extract from notes made on an inspection of the diary.

Klüpfel visited Panigot, Tesson Mill and Victoria Inn and in notes referring to these visits there is a sinister inference to be drawn from the comment 'house above Victoria tunnel'. Is this to draw to the attention of those who would use his notes the convenience of an existing building above the tunnel, as was recorded in Auschwitz?

The text of Michael Ginns' book ('Archive book No 7' being the alternative title) is outstanding in its details, thoroughness and depth of research.

Unconsciously Mr Ginns has provided some detail which supports the gaschamber/crematorium thesis.

For example ... on page 11 we find ... (in referring to excavation methods)

"the 60cm gauge railway lines that had been employed to remove the rubble; these then formed the basis of the eventual internal transport system".

For bodies perhaps?

then again ...

"the liquid concrete '...was poured by way of a chute down the embryo escape shaft".

The same procedure was used in the building of the Birkenau Crematoriums."

Then again, when commenting upon the construction of Ho. 1 (Munition Store 1) we find the following ...

"This was all contained in the lined chambers which lie at right-angles to the primary gallery, being immediately accessible from the

unloading platform which incorporates a 60cm gauge railway track. Beneath the platform run the ducts of a very comprehensive drainage system"

A similar unloading platform was installed in Auschwitz from which walked the prisoners down steps (see page 139) the railway track and the drainage ducts are also there for the periodic washing down.

Of equal interest are the comments on page 141 in reference to Ho 8 on the **Festpistah** Map which refers to the tunnel as **Artillerieunterkunft.** This is the tunnel later used as a Casualty Receiving Station during the latter weeks of the war.

As with those in Birkenau, Ho 8 is singular in that it is the only tunnel in Jersey entirely devoid of curves, all corners being right angles. The floor, in common with other tunnels, slopes towards the entrances.

It will be noted that the blueprint of Krematorium 2 at Auschwitz also shows a construction consisting entirely of right angle corners.

There is a description in the book which reads as follows:

"The railway system vanishes under blank walls, a situation brought about when the complex was converted from artillery workshops into a hospital and the ends of unfinished galleries were bricked up and converted into wards".

Were the 'wards' for eventual conversion into gassing chambers? The rail track is laid down one side of the ward and a drainage channel on the opposite side.

These would be the requirements in a highly systemised crematorium such as was designed for Birkenau.

Right angled corners would of course have been necessary to make for ease of fitting gas-proof doors to each of the chambers.

Undoubtedly the most authoritative book written about the Auschwitz/Birkenau gaschambers, in fact the whole study of 'gassing' and 'incineration' as the most efficient means of genocide is that written by Jean-Claude Pressac (New York: published by the Beate Klarsfeld Foundation

1989) under the title *'AUSCHWITZ: technique and operation of the gaschambers"*.

The book is dedicated to Peter S Kalikow in honour of his work on the New York Memorial to the Holocaust, one of 15 such Memorials spread throughout the United States, whereas **not one** exists in Britain.

Mr Ben Helfgott who is chairman of Yad Vashem, the Museum of the Holocaust in Jerusalem, would like to see a Memorial to the Holocaust in Britain.

As already remarked, gassing as a method of mass murder was progressive. As described in Jean-Claude Pressac's book 86 Jews were murdered in August 1943 in Struthof by mixing a measure of prussic acid with controlled quantities of water.

On this occasion as an example of the German fascination with thoroughness, all the details of the operation were recorded following an established procedure.

a) the volume of the fumigated rooms:

(Note: for 'fumigated' read "rooms in which gas was used"). Note how euphemisms are being used. An early admission of the need to suppress the truth.

b) Amount of Zyclon B used.

c) Name of fumigation official in charge.

d) Names of other personnel involved in the operation.

e) Time required for gas to take effect.

f) Time at which 'disinfected' rooms were 'released'. (i.e., when the bodies were removed) *** There is a manufacturer's 'recommendation' attached suggesting a minimum of 20 hours. An open admission that the manufacturers knew the purpose for which the product would be used.

There is a plan in the book (the original must have undergone every possible technical treatment to obtain the best results when printed) but it is indistinct.

This is not surprising as such plans, blueprints and documents had remained stored in the Moscow archives for 45 years or more before being released for public view.

There is some documentary evidence that a request was submitted to Central Headquarters in Berlin for more 'delousing' buildings (i.e. gaschambers).

Gaschamber dimensions have been estimated from photographs in the book, based on sizes of doors and windows and the slope of the roof at Kanada I the approximate sizes being:

length 30-35' x 20' wide x 9' high*

* if a ceiling is incorporated which from photos discovered it would seem there was.

BUNKER 2 (subsequently called Bunker V) and referred to as 'White House' incorporated four gaschambers of differing sizes with an overall floor area of 105 square metres plus two 'undressing' sheds.

At Alter Fajnzylberb 12 bodies were allegedly handled at a time but study of the situation would indicate that only 5 would have been practicable. Yet a further indication of the desire of those operating these 'establishments' to please their masters by exaggeration.

Furnaces had to be cleaned every evening and a hoped for target of incineration time of 80 minutes was registered plus a 20 minutes cooling off period.

In the Trezebinia labour camp the original size of the gaschamber was 78.2 square metres or a chamber approximately 25' x 10' (See Krematorium 1 : January 1945)

Pressac, in his book, expresses some surprise that the industrial extermination of the Jews at Auschwitz/Birkenau was not put into practice until June/August 42 and not implemented until March/June 43, but as already remarked, problems were constantly arising.

Topf was not the only Company involved in tendering for the manufacture of the ovens. Tenders for the building of

Krematorium 2 'plant' , as it was called, were submitted by Huta and by Lenz & Co., both of Kattewitz. Topf obtained the contract. A specialist firm of builders was employed, this company being Robert Kaehler of Myslowitz.

On pages 228/9 of Pressac's book there are pictures of manhole entrances with access ladders almost identical to those found in Michael Ginn's book of photographs of the Channel Islands tunnels. The size of the air-ducting in the chambers was 20 centimetres square.

In order to maintain the 'calm' nature of these operations and to deter panic when groups were being prepared for gassing some 'genuine' delousing chambers were introduced where the prisoners were taken, told to strip, leaving their clothes outside for delousing. The prisoners were then put through a delousing process and on emerging were kitted out with 'clean' clothing and let loose in the compound to 'spread the word'. This being yet a further example of the duplicity and deviousness of the minds behind the scheme in which everyone was involved.

Ovens which were in use required cleaning out both in the actual furnaces where, of course, clinker formed and in the base where the ashes of the corpses accumulated and had to be raked out.

In some cases corpses were put on a 'roller' conveying system (still to be seen at Auschwitz today) thus facilitating the speed and ease with which the corpses were fed into the furnaces. The moving parts were operating under conditions of intense heat and regular breakdowns occurred.

Although never introduced one oven designer, Sauder, submitted a blueprint for a unique crematorium furnace based on the production line principle.

Sauder's design allows for 'everything' taking place **inside** the furnace itself. The firebox is at the bottom. The corpses would have been introduced at the top, one or two at a time, and would slowly have slid down three inclined refractory grids under their own weight arriving at the bottom as ashes.

No moving parts would have been required the corpses disintegrating with the heat.

The rough dimensions of such a construction would have been: 2m wide x 2.5m deep (top) to 3m deep (base) x 6m high. The idea never got beyond the drawing board.

Photos by Michel Folco were discovered of the Topf coke fired 'double-muffle' (in other words an oven taking two bodies at once) which had been installed under the 'New Hospital' of Mauthausen KL.

Sturmbannfuhrer or SS Major Rudolf Hoess was for a period of time Camp Commandant at Auschwitz/Birkenau, and in one of the documents discovered under his name he records the unlikely figure of 900 people squeezed into an area 78.2m square. In other words approx 15625 sq. ft or a chamber approx 150' x 100'.

Pressac infers, without committing himself, that such a large figure is unlikely, calculations however indicate that it would be possible but hardly practicable. Smaller rooms or chambers with the same density of souls to the square yard had proved more manageable.

The German fascination with thoroughness and accuracy created conflict in the minds of many Civil and Military Nazi officials of middle and upper echelons for whilst they were anxious to appear exact in their record keeping they were also anxious to appear successful in their duties with the result that whilst records were kept with apparently strict observance to detail they might be exaggerated or diminished accordance to the requirements of the occasion.

This led to an almost naive approach to investigation and study of records by the British Intelligence Units, the report by Major Cotton on the situation he found in Alderney in 1945 following the liberation of the Channel Islands, being an example (see pages {...}).

One such is the report submitted on the Auschwitz/ Birkenau gassings by SS Major Alfred Franke-Gricksch, adjutant to the SS General Maximilian Von Herff.

Franke-Gricksch had visited Krematorium II and witnessed the gassing of 2930 Greek Jews from the Salonika Ghetto. His report, submitted to his Chief Von Herff and for Reichfuhrer SS Himmler was entitled "The Jewish Resettlement Action", a useful German euphemism for the murdering of Jews, and to be remembered when considering the name which would have been given to the removal of the 450,000 Jews in Britain when shipping them to the Channel Islands.

The general tenor of Franke-Gricksch's voluminous report was evidently justifying his visit and increasing his personal stature. He reports that "the 'titling' of the operation – which was his own idea – was significant in obtaining the cooperation of the intended victims".

He reports that 300/400 people fall asleep in one minute. Allowing for time for the gas to be extracted by the air extraction plant, the corpses are then dragged immediately from one chamber to another where heads are shaved (for hair) and teeth extracted (for gold or jewel content). This operation was conducted by prisoners under the supervision of armed guards. A photograph of this work in progress is in Jean-Claude Pressac's book.

'Prepared' corpses were then loaded on to a lift, he tells us, which takes them to 10 big crematorium furnaces in which the corpses are burned.

Apparently with some relish he explains that 'fresh' corpses burn particularly well, the whole process requiring only 1/2 to 1 Zentnér (25-50kg) of coke".

"The present capacity of the 'resettlement action' furnaces" ... he claims "is 10,000 in 24 hours, the result of this action being 500,000 Jews". We do not know if Franke-Gricksch was promoted!

This is of course a complete fabrication in order to gain his report notice and acclamation.

Pressac argues that the true figure would much more likely have been 3000, a figure close to that estimated in this book.

Many of the reproductions of the drawings and blueprints lack essential detail having faded and having been prepared by the SS in a hurry or by Jewish prisoners who saw no reason for truth or accuracy in what they were doing, except that it justified their existence for a few more days.

For some reason of which there is no record the openings through which the Zyclon B pellets were inserted were enlarged from 30/40cm to 40/50cm.

One of the problems which caused delays and redesigning was the discovery that whilst the multi-ovens were efficient and speedy the heat generated caused overheating of the chimneys and disintegration of bricks and cracks (risse) appeared in the furnace.

It would appear that as one problem was solved yet another arose, there is a report of serious damage, at one stage, to Krematorium 4.

When constructing the gaschambers with additional chimneys (presumably to achieve heat distribution) civilian workers employed by the construction company Riedel & Son openly referred to the building's western most room as 'the gaschambers'. This is recorded on 2nd March 1943 and is further evidence that German civilians knew what was going on.

On page 465-469 of Jean-Claude Pressac's book there is further evidence of how 'prisoners' were forced or encouraged by the offer of special privileges to work against their own.

Once the four Krematoria were almost finished a specialised group of prisoners were enlisted to 'tend' the maintenance of the 'plant'. There was a total of 900 of them and they were given the special title of ...

'The Sonderkommando'

They were fortunate in that whilst a 'Sonderkommando; it was, unless you fell ill, security against being one of those who would be selected for gassing.

However, evidently sickened by what they were involved in and being involved in the extermination of their own kind there was a revolt in the early days of September 1944.

Two hundred of them were gassed on the 7th September and on the 7th October five hundred were shot, whilst a further 100 were taken away and never seen again.

There is no record that the idea of a 'Sonderkommando' was pursued. It is only possible to guess that as with other camps the utilisation of the fittest amongst the prisoners for the job became the answer.

There was for a time, whilst the super-Krematoria were being built, a policy operating in the Auschwitz/Birkenau Camp which required arrival parties of 200 or less to be shot. As the ovens proved, initially, less efficient than hoped for, this was increased to 300. Crematoria 1 and 2 were processing 2000 souls each whilst Crematoria 3 and 4 were handling 1000 with the 'Bunker' accounting for a further 1000.

The chambers holding 1000 souls were proving too large and eventually it would seem that the ideal size of a chamber was approximately 10m long x 4m wide (i.e. 32' x 13') a size matching many of the chambers in the Jersey and Guernsey tunnels.

The 'Leichenkeller 1' of Krematorium II and III were 30m long by 7m wide and 2.44m high, similar in size to the Guernsey chambers. It is interesting to note that the 'Leichenkellers' were later divided into two.

Finally, there is the unsolved mystery of the blocked tunnels in both Islands. It should be remembered that from D-Day to the day of liberation the Nazis had eleven months in which to destroy evidence. Almost to the day of liberation the Wermacht behaved as though the war would continue and guards were maintained on installations including tunnel entrances. Civilians, were not permitted anywhere near them consequently they had no knowledge of what was in the tunnels.

When the British Army arrived they began work on the tunnels in almost indecent haste removing large stocks of German military equipment but there were some tunnels which were blown up and sealed off almost immediately.

The explanation offered for this was that the equipment was in very poor condition and of no use, not worth removing or destroying, so they buried it.

Over the years a great deal of machinery had been brought into the Islands and used for the excavations.

One piece of machinery, especially if dismantled, looks like another, therefore it is possible that the 'machinery' lying in the inaccessible tunnels was not 'machinery' but the ovens and equipment for the establishment of the crematoria.

Is this some of the information still being kept 'under wraps' until 2045.

*Sylt, the S.S. Concentration Camp on Alderney
after the Nazis had destroyed the evidence before escaping in 1945.*

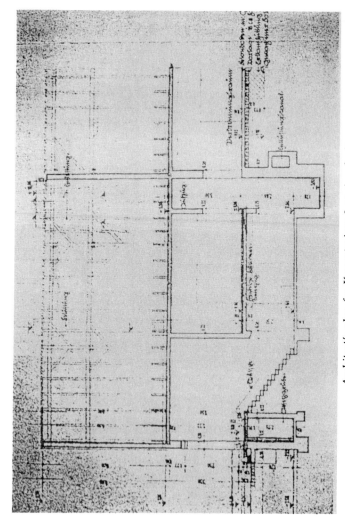

Architect's plan for Krematorium 2 at Auschwitz, showing stairs and chute (bottom left). Later, the chute was removed.

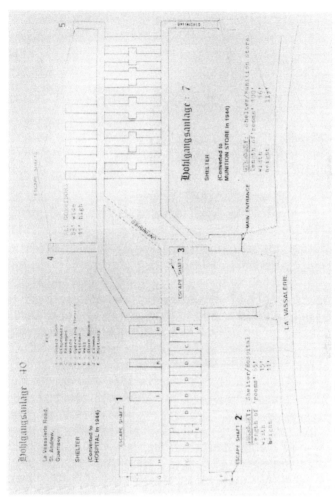

Ground Plan of German underground Hospital and Ammunition Store,
GUERNSEY

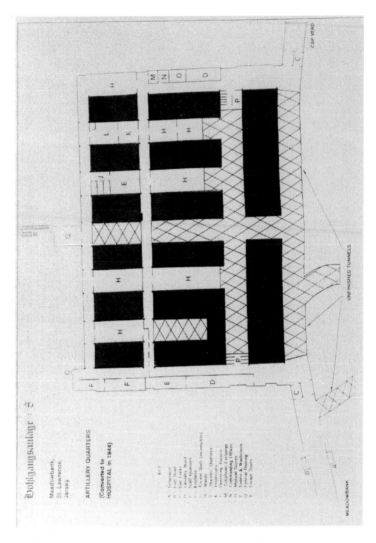

*Ground Plan of German underground Artillery Quarters,
JERSEY, later converted to a Hospital*

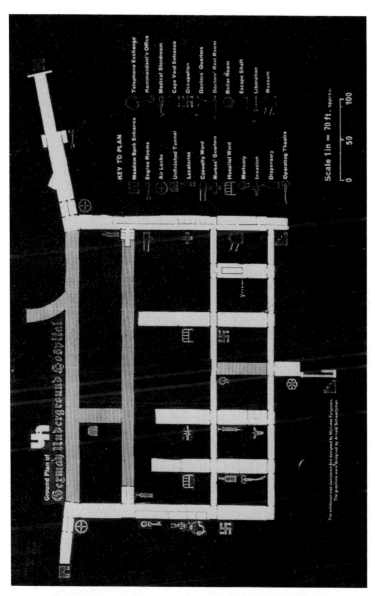

Ground Plan of German underground Hospital, JERSEY

*Two-tier wooden bunks with straw mattresses as they would have been
in the tunnels reserved for prisoners fit enough to work
in the gaschambers and the crematoria on Jersey and Guernsey*

THE SUMMING UP

World War II as with all wars, brought with it the break down of social behaviour in whatever form it had existed in whatever country the war touched.

In the Channel Islands, a natural prison when freedom is denied, it was not surprising that collaboration with the enemy appeared excessive, especially to those part of the daily life.

It is well to remember in relation to this situation that by 1944, 42% of the French population was, directly or indirectly, working for the German war machine.

In the Channel Islands, at least, the discipline of the ordinary German soldier is to this day still commended. It was the indoctrinated Nazi soldier, the SS and the Gestapo and the evil personalities who filled the vacuum created by an evil regime who should never be forgiven or forgotten, and many of those men are alive and free today.

Like weeds, which, if chopped off at the head reappear stronger than ever, they should be torn out by the roots and disposed of.

In Jersey and Guernsey, contrary to the many stories told otherwise, the degree of resistance, in view of the circumstances, was remarkable. Some of these stories are told by Mrs Brockley and by Mr Joe Miere. There are the tales of brave Jersey ladies who, at the risk of being shot or being sent to a concentration camp sheltered escapees, not for a night, but for days and weeks on end.

In Guernsey 'V' signs appeared everywhere at one time, and a brave Guernsey lady, Mrs Winifred Green was imprisoned for four months for saying 'Heil Churchill'. She spent two weeks in a Guernsey jail and was then shipped to Caen where, in the same prison, she met Mrs Lillian Kinnaird and Mrs Kathleen le Norman. They had been sent to Caen, because, according to Mr Joe Miere, who was himself imprisoned for seven months, the prisons were overflowing with men and women who had annoyed the Germans. Mr Delauney, Mr Ogier and Mr de Guillebon were only three of many more who suffered imprisonment for pin-prick crimes.

It is well to remember that these were **ordinary** people.

.If the Germans were to maintain discipline such small crimes had to be punished. They were too minor to merit deportation to a concentration camp, so the prisons were full. There was even a waiting list to go to prison, so who can say the ordinary Islander did not resist to the best of his or her ability?

Mrs Louise Gould was arrested in June 1944 for sheltering an escaped Russian, sentenced to two years imprisonment and sent to Revensbrück Concentration Camp where she died in 1945 ... gassed.

Arrested for involvement in the same incident was Mrs Gould's brother, Harold Le Druillenec. He was sent to Belsen and was the only Briton to survive the horrors of that camp.

Mr Le Druillenec died about 11 years ago.

Rene Le Mottee has also since died and Augusta Metcalf. Still full of memories of those days are Stella Perkins, Leonard Perkins, Norman le Brocq and Robert Le Sueur. All were punished for assisting the escape of Russian and Ukrainian prisoners and all were honoured in 1965 by the Soviet Government for their work and their bravery with gold watches.

The British Government has still done nothing to recognise their bravery.

This list is far from complete and there are some who prefer to remain unmentioned.

There are of course those who wonder why the bravery and loyalty of these people has not been recognised by the British Government. There was the magnanimous reason offered by one recipient of a Russian award who said "well, we were helping Russians not Britons", but surely, were these brave people not fighting a common enemy?

If the Bailiff deserved a Lordship did not ordinary resistance fighters, some of whom were arrested and sent to Concentration Camps deserve some form of recognition?

What of those who died for their patriotism?

Whilst every excuse, every reasonable argument, may be raised to defend the difficulties of carrying out an effective resistance campaign in the confines of a small island, when compared with the greater opportunities in countries such as France, Holland and Denmark there is little doubt that the degree of willing, almost enthusiastic collaboration given by the Influential of the Islands to the German Occupying Forces was well in excess of what can be considered as inevitable, reasonable and acceptable in the circumstances.

If such an assessment would seem unfair then why were twelve cases passed to the Director of Public Prosecutions by an Investigating Civil Affairs Unit? **No action was taken but it happened** and is probably the reason why the files were put on a 'secret' and 'hold' list until 2045!

Attempts at 'pin-prick' resistance by the ordinary Islanders were punished severely, almost enthusiastically, by the Guernsey Authorities and faithfully reported back to their German 'masters'.

It would seem, on examining all aspects of the probable reasons for the withholding of files and the 'tampering' with files from the Guernsey Archives, which received so much publicity in 1992, that there can be only one answer and that is the reluctance by the British and Guernsey Authorities to admit to the rest of the world, and to those who endangered their lives as resistance workers, that the Guernsey Authorities and some rank and file Guernseymen worked as hard on behalf of the Nazis as any other conquered administration in Western Europe.

Was a 'deal' done with the Nazi murderers on Alderney and in Guernsey which went well beyond the limits of enforced and unavoidable cooperation? Was the safety of the Nazi murderers guaranteed in exchange for silence? Is that why they have not been tried? Might these criminals, under public interrogation quote behaviour, equal to their own, by some Guernseymen? Did one or two of the Island authorities themselves start behaving as brutally as their Nazi masters?

An interesting 'side light' on these events is that the then Bailiff of Guernsey Mr Victor Carey, was knighted for his 'services to the country' when war ceased!

Poor muddled Major Ambrose Sherwill on whom fell more than a fair share of the responsibilities when it was too late to put them right, was also knighted as was Mr. John Leale.

But strong minded Mr A M Coutanche, Bailiff of Jersey, who quietly and determinedly fought the Germans every inch of the way throughout the Occupation deservedly became a Lord.

The contrast in the behaviour and attitude of the Administrating Authorities of the two Islands and the effect strong leadership has upon a population affords an opportunity for study by those interested.

And so the mystery of the secret files remain.

Probably the biggest mystery is why they have to remain a mystery when so much can be deduced from what is already known.

It is unlikely that factual proof will ever be found to confirm the belief that the 'underground hospitals' would have been converted to gaschambers yet there is more circumstantial evidence to prove that it **was** so than to prove that it was not.

That the Nazis, had they won the war, would have extended the Final Solution to Britain is without doubt. All that is needed is an understanding of their convictions and their beliefs.

That the Channel Islands would have been the perfect solution to carrying out such an operation and that they would have become over the years the extermination site for the whole of Europe becomes a logical prognosis.

That the effort to bring Nazi war criminals to justice must continue till they are all found and convicted or have died there is no doubt for these were the indoctrinated Nazi Youth of the war years whose ideas and beliefs are infecting the youth of today.

It is hoped this book will contribute towards that effort and that justice will be restored.

POSTSCRIPT

Item 1

Almost immediately after the war some 200,000 East Europeans were invited into Britain. Many of them were escapees from SS units who had joined the Red Army pretending to be escaped prisoners from the Camps. Others were believed to be dissidents escaping arrest by the Soviet. Despite the fact that the USSR had been allies during the war British Government antipathy and distrust towards the Russians remained. Most of the 200,000 were not screened.

Despite subsequent MI5 investigations proving them to be ex-Nazis of various East European nationalities and German, numbers of them are still sheltering in this country under British nationality.

Item 2

Erich Priebke, one of the men named in this book as a suspected war criminal for crimes in Italy has lived for 50 years in Bariloche, a town in Argentina, where **almost all of the population is ex or pro-Nazi.** Priebke is under deportation request to face trial in Italy.

Item 3

What was the fascination of Hitler for women? Hundreds of them wrote to him and sent him presents or offered to bear his child.

Item 4

Richard Dimbleby, the famous wartime broadcaster, David Dimbleby's father, and dubbed 'The Voice of Brittain' was one of the first reporters to enter Belsen with Brittish troops. His

155

famous 'Belsen Broadcast' about the frightfulness he found there was not believed by the BBC radio executives and they tried to stop the broadcast. Richard Dimbleby threatened a public resignation if they did not do so. It was broadcast.

Yet another example of the British Establishment refusing to believe the stories of the Nazi camps.

Item 5

As early as 1941 Jan Karski, a Pole, was horrified to learn of and see the atrocities perpetrated against the Jews. At great risk to his life he gathered evidence and in 1942 placed that evidence before Officials in London and America. In both countries his information was rejected, ignored or treated with derision and disbelief. The story of the dangers he endured to obtain the evidence and his efforts to convince Governments is told in a book *'Karski – how one man tried to stop the Holocaust'* by E Thomas Wood and Stanislaw M Jankowski.

Item 6

Victory for the Allies after D-Day in 1945 hung in the balance. V2 bombs had already dropped on London. The fact that there was no defence against these supersonic bombs was kept from the public to avoid panic.

The Allied advance was slow. They were only just in time – a matter of a few weeks – to prevent the launch of thousands of V2 bombs from Holland which would have flattened London and almost certainly have led to our capitulation.

The V2 bombs were made in Mount Kohnstein mentioned in this book.

Item 7

If the V2 bomb had not succeeded an even greater threat was being planned by Hitler, according to British nuclear power expert Philip Henshaw. Apparently Germany had prepared radio-active waste with the intention of producing a nuclear bomb.

In order to ensure the safety of the production process Japan agreed to make the radioactive material, which was despatched by sea, into a bomb. The bomb would have been returned to Germany by submarine.

Item 8

'One of the biggest military disasters of all time' were the words used by Canadian Brigadier Churchill Mann to describe the assault upon Dieppe in 1942 when only 1250 Canadian soldiers returned out of 5000.

Mountbatten described the event as 'a great victory' and 'think of the lessons we learnt'. It was yet another of those disasters in which Mountbatten was to have a hand and in which his ineptitude and incompetence and disregard for the lives of others was evident.

Like Richard Dimbleby whose on the spot reporting was being repeatedly smothered so was Frank Gillard's report on the Dieppe raid. Both these men were brilliant reporters, both suffered the most severe censorship, and both believed the public should have been told the truth.

Item 9

Neo-Nazis have not been slow to realise the possibilities of computers in the spread and revival of the Nazi doctrines.

Computer super-highways have been infiltrated world wide by underground cyber-Nazis in Austria and Germany, recruiting for neo-Nazi groups has been going on for almost two years.

Advice on the preparation of bomb manufacture is common. For more secret communications an American scrambling system named FGP is allowing the use of their system.

Also through the 'super-highways' system, computer 'games' aimed at children and teenagers will shortly be available in Britain. These games include the propagation of Nazi theories of genocide, ethnic cleansing and the glorification of Hitler, Nazism and the Aryan race.

THE TESTIMONIES

Introduction to the Testimonies

So far as it has been possible without exposing the reader to boredom through repetition or irritation with the grammatical form I have endeavoured to leave the contributor's texts just as they happened, in their natural delivery.

Three of the four Testimonies were recorded on tape and each lasted well over one and one half hours from which it will be realised a good deal of editing was required. I hope the Testimonies have not suffered for that reason.

In the case of Vassili Marempolski the portion used came from his book of memoirs given to the Author, and written in his native Ukrainian. I hope it has not suffered in the translation. For example the word 'mine' has been left unaltered when the word 'tunnel' was meant.

Each narrative is a tale of courage, determination and fortitude, of harrowing experiences and sights which would leave an adult with memories likely to be the breeding ground of ever recurring nightmares.

But Mrs. Brockley was not an adult ... she was only six when her home was straffed by the Luftwaffe and the Germans goose-stepped into Jersey. On the same day Tommy Syms was only eight. Margaret Brockley was eleven when she was herself starving and competing with starving German Soldiers collecting acorns and scavenging for scraps to eat in the months before liberation.

Margaret Brockley had not been encouraged to tell her story until I met her, but quickly realised she had a sympathetic ear and an understanding audience.

159

Once the flood gates of vivid memories had been opened the pent up emotions of years poured out unchecked... words came tumbling after one another in an uninterrupted cascade.

It may be argued that such detailed, expressive memories are unlikely in such young persons. That may be true under normal circumstances but those who have experienced the heightened awareness which seems to be the product of war fever will concede that in a deeply responsible person, no matter what age, no matter what the experience, good or bad, such experiences are etched upon the memory and need only to be conjured from the subconscious.

It is such memories, expressed in words, spoken in sorrow, hatred, fear and joy which have been recorded here.

In vivid contrast to Margaret Brockley's story are the almost matter-of-fact staccato phrases of Vassili Marempolski, hiding the indomitable courage of a sensitive young man, only fifteen, torn from his family and his country, beaten, starved, tortured, in daily fear for his life, surviving from day to day and carrying in his heart and mind the dream of returning to his Motherland, as each day he is worked to the edge of exhaustion and watches his companions beaten to death.

Vassili Marempolski was until recently a lecturer in Ukrainian poetry at the Zaporozhye University. He tells the story of his lost youthful years.

Joe Miere who was 15 when he first saw German soldiers has retained a remarkable degree of tolerance and compassion towards those who held him prisoner in his own Island, whereas

Tommy Syms who was ten when sent to Biberach Concentration Camp, a most vulnerable age, had his youth shattered and has been trying to rebuild his life ever since.

Meeting any one of these people today, fifty years on, as with so many others, it is difficult to imagine the fear felt, the privations suffered and the sights observed. Such people are the unseen, unnoticed casualties of war.

CRSO

MARGARET BROCKLEY'S TESTIMONY
(Abridged version)

I was born in Jersey in 1935 and it was my 6th birthday when the Germans jackbooted into Jersey in July 1941.

We had been told the Germans were coming. We had had leaflets dropped but we didn't really believe it. We were sitting having our Sunday lunch when we heard the sound of planes. I ran upstairs to the bedroom and looked out. I could see what seemed like hundreds of silver fish glistening in the sky. I called my Mother to come and look. She said she didn't know whether they were ours or German.

At the time we were living not far from the docks. We had just started eating when a plane swooped down and started machine gunning. My Mother cried out 'under the table', and there we stayed with our meal getting cold until the planes had gone.

Our neighbour, who lived in the same row of cottages, came to tell us after the planes had left, that he had seen his mate blown up under one of the lorries down at the docks.

It wasn't long before another group of planes came over. This time they dropped more leaflets stating the terms they were coming on. If we didn't comply they would bomb and strafe again. The leaflets said every house in the Island must display a white flag by a certain time.

We went up the steps by the cottages and there watched people putting out bits of white cloth from their windows. The street was festooned with what was supposed to be white flags but you have never seen such insults in your life. Dirty knickers, dirty nappies, old bits of cloth, anything people could find to insult them.

When they finally arrived they had to walk up through that.

I said to my Mother... 'How long are they going to stay?'. She said... 'Oh! ninety days, there's a good Geneva convention, this is an open city, the Militia and the troops have left, there's nobody armed here, they should be out in ninety days.' But they stayed right through the war.

After all that the adults, who were my Mother, my Grand-mother, my Mother's sister and my Mother's brother, had a good talk and decided to leave because we were afraid, like a lot of other people.

My Uncle had left the Island with his wife six months earlier convinced the Germans would come. He had emptied his big house, left us the key and asked us to look after it.

Now we too were leaving, before the Germans arrived.

We each took a small suitcase and whatever clothes we could wear and went down to the quay but when we got there, there were crowds of people all jostling one another, shouting and crying, and the only boat visible was one small tug already packed with people and lots of children. A man said to my Mother, he seemed to be in charge, 'There is no room for you but send the kids'.

My Mother pushed her way through, grabbing us by the hand and got close to the tug crying, 'for God's sake take the children'. I can remember the tears streaming down her face and the desperate way she held us to her before passing us up to the people on the boat.

I remember looking back and seeing my Grand-mother prostrate on the ground and Mother leaning over her. The boat was about to be cast off when I realised I could not leave her, so I screamed and screamed and fought and said to the people around me 'Put me back', 'Put me back', 'I won't go' and I started to climb on to the side. Someone said 'all right, pass her back' and before I knew what was happening both I and my brother were once more standing on the quay.

In my childlike mind I thought we were better off with the family than going off into the unknown on that horrible dirty boat. My Grand-mother recovered sufficiently for us to get home and it was wonderful to be all together again.

Five days after that we moved into my Uncle's house. It was huge and had a large garden with facilities to grow food and to keep rabbits and chickens.

We heard later that the reason why there was only one boat, was because the Baliff, Mr Coutanche, in order to stop a panic evacuation of the Island, which he thought was not necessary, had told some of the ships to return empty. There were many who never forgave him for that, although he did try very hard throughout the Occupation to help everyone.

We quickly discovered that if all the rooms in the house were not furnished in a way which made them look occupied that the Germans would commandeer them for billeting purposes. My Mother and Grand-mother had decided they must do two things – fill the rooms with furniture and buy as much food as possible to stock away in hiding because they knew there would be shortages. So they sold everything possible to raise money. My Mother even sold her wedding ring.

The Germans were intent on billeting as many soldiers as possible with Islanders so that were we bombed by the British, civilians would be killed too. Furniture was easy to get cheaply, but food began to become scarce as soon as the German troops started shopping. They bought everything in sight to send home. Our own shopping expeditions had made us broke but we had the things with which to survive, or so we thought.

Our school was only just around the corner. We had Jersey teachers. Later on the Germans began to insist we were taught German and from time to time sent round inspectors demanding to see specimens of the work. This became difficult. Paper became very scarce and finally we had a consignment from France which was graph paper, very cheap stuff. We had pencils and rubbers and we had to draw or write quite lightly on the paper, do our work and then rub it out again. This happened over and over until the paper became too thin to use. When **that** ran out we used slates, roof slates, and chalk, and when the chalk ran out we used brick, but we still managed to learn and, I at least, did not fall behind with my education.

One of the things my Grand-mother was very clever over was the way she kept her collection of sovereigns until their price on the black market was extortionate, the proceeds from those went on food too.

Every now and then the Germans raided us to see what food we had but it was such a big house and garden it was fairly easy to hide things.

Within six months they had introduced rationing and this was what we got...

Bread	4 lbs 10 ozs
Meat	3 or 4 ozs
Sugar	3 or 4 ozs
Butter	4 ozs
Cooking fat	2 ozs
Salt	1 to 3 ozs
Coffee substitute	1 to 2 ozs
Flour or Macaroni or oats	6 ozs
Potatoes	5 lbs
Separated Milk	3 and a half pints

This was what we were **supposed** to get but there were times when shortages, because the Germans commandeered the best and the troops bought yet more on the black market and clandestinely from shopkeepers, became so great we were at starvation level. To counteract this my Grand-mother taught my Mother to grow tobacco which she then sold on the black market to buy food.

I remember being hungry all the time and my little brother used to cry because he couldn't have things he liked and couldn't understand.

The Germans had turned Victoria College into a canteen and a store place for food. Victoria College was only just down the road from us so my brother and I used to go down and sit on the steps with an old soldier. He was lovely to children. He was terribly worried his wife and children in

Dresden might have been killed from the bombing. He used to give us mugs of hot soup with meat in it. Something we never had at home. He also gave us bread from his own ration. One day we went home with a piece of bread each and my Uncle said 'Where did you get that?' so we told him. He said 'You didn't steal it from them?'. 'No. They gave it to us'. So he took us both by the ear and said ' You take nothing, nothing, from them. They have invaded us, taken everything we had, and now hand it out to us like paupers... you give it them back. I'll see you starve first'. And he made us give it back.

When we returned he said 'Now... if you want that bread go off and steal, get what you can from them, but steal'.

When rations got very short we would queue for hours or go down to the soup kitchens where we would get grated carrots, or some watery soup with a bit of pepper in it, or a swede grated. It was all horrible but one was so hungry anything would do. The queues would be anything from a quarter of a mile to half a mile, just to get some watery soup.

From time to time shipments came from France. The Germans always took the best and the rubbish came on the market for us. One day a boat arrived from France with apples and cherries. My brother and I managed to get some half rotten cherries. We were so happy we ran to a closed shop with a second floor balcony. We were laughing and trying to spit the pips as far as possible into the street. One of my pips fell on an Officer's cap. He was furious and chased us, and I was taken to the Army Head-quarters. My brother ran away and told my Mother. My Mother was distraught for she didn't know where I was. I spent three hours being questioned. I was very frightened, because I thought they would put me in prison. Eventually my Mother arrived and remonstrated with the Officers and they let me go with a caution.

We always managed to get a tip off when they were coming to inspect the house. We had chickens and rabbits, quite a few chickens, so when they were coming we would all dash to the run, grab the chickens, tie their legs and beaks – with the exception of half a dozen... and put them into a prepared pit near the compost heap. The pit was prepared with straw in the bottom. We would cover it with a piece of corrugated then put the compost and rubbish on top. All they saw were a few scrawny chickens and some rabbits. They used to take a rabbit or two but that wasn't too bad. They were not tame, domestic rabbits, but wild ones we had caught and bred in cages. It was dangerous really because some of them had myxomatosis.

Although my Uncle was so severe about us not accepting food from the Germans we still continued to do so. This we did at night. My Mother used to lock us in at night but we would escape through the window, go down the back garden over the garage roof and by a short rope drop into Le Breton Lane.

This was all after curfew which lasted until about 6 or 7 in the morning.

Fritz used to leave food for us in a shed with a small window not far from the College. Standing on my brothers shoulders I used to lean in and take out what Fritz had left. We would take it home, hide it and then next morning tell my Mother and Uncle we had stolen it. Had we been caught I suppose we would have got everyone into trouble but we didn't think of that at the time.

I said the school had been taken over by the Germans. They billeted there, in the upstairs floors and down below they stabled the Belgian horses. There was no carpet in the hall so you could hear them walking through and the horses stamping at night.

Food was getting very short and we were very grateful for that given to us by Fritz but that began to change late in 1942. The ordinary soldiers were sent back to Europe and Nazi soldiers came instead. We had had a reasonable sort of Kommandant for the first eighteen months but with the arrival of the Nazi youth the attitude of everyone changed.

They were arrogant and many behaved in a disgusting way towards people including the children. We soon learned to give them a wide berth, and of course the food supply stopped.

We heard stories of a house being taken over by them, with a beautifully frescoed dining room being stripped out.

Life became very hard and acts of petty sabotage or demonstrations of contempt for the Germans resulted in severe reprisals.

Once we had our water cut off for weeks and we were forced to use stand pipes. Some had to walk miles to a stand pipe to collect two buckets of water. How the old people got on I don't know. They used to cut off the electricity too.

We were luckier than many for we had an old black stove with an oven in which we burned all the rubbish. We also had two pumps drawing water from wells inside the house but it wasn't fit for drinking. We always covered them up when the Germans came.

Washing was a difficulty because soap was more or less non-existent. You could get stuff on the black market. It looked like a cake of soap but all it was was a blob of something to hold together a gritty substance, perhaps it was sand. It smelt horrible.

When my Mother and Grand-mother had been stocking up they had bought quantities of Parazone and soap and candles, but by 1943 these were running short.

In June of 1942 an order was issued that all wirelesses must be surrendered, but we hid ours and it was never found.

I remember my family being very upset when in May three boys tried to escape to England. Everything went wrong, one was drowned, the remaining two were imprisoned but one, Maurice Gould, died later in a prison camp.

This was an unhappy time because in September some of our friends who were English were deported to Germany.

With the arrival of the new Kommandant things became much more difficult but Bailiff Coutanche worked hard mediating for the local people who were begining to suffer from the arrival of the Nazi Youth.

One day I heard my Mother talking about a neighbour. We had not seen him for days then news came that he was part of a forced labour group recently formed. This was a new innovation evidently brought in to boost slave labour which we knew they had been using.

I was down near the docks. There were barricades of barbed wire and trestles and two sentries.

We could look across to where the weighbridge was and only one sentry. My brother and I had been watching all morning the coming and going from the boats. We couldn't get down to the dock but we could see quite well from where we had climbed. About fifty yards back there was another barricade. No one was allowed beyond that but we'd passed the one and they hadn't stopped us, so we pressed on. They seemed not to bother as we were children. One of the things they used to say was 'Rause kleine kinden' (clear of young children) but we didn't take any notice. This particular sentry must have seen us but he didn't take any notice and went to the other end of the barricade. He just turned his back on us, and left us there.

From off one of the ships I saw something that stays with me to this day. It horrified me so deeply. It was terrible. There must have been about 30 people came from one of the ships. I found out later they were Russians. There were all kinds of people. There were men, there were women, and there were small children some the same age as me. They were all in rags. They looked terribly tired and their feet were the things that I looked at. We used to run barefoot a lot of the time but their feet were wrapped up in rags soaked with blood and cake dried blood where they had been made to walk. Their clothes hung about them and they looked utterly drained. Their eyes looked dead and there was one old man being pushed and shoved along. He must have been 80ish but looked more. He had white hair and a white beard like old Father Time. To my childish mind it seemed the longest beard

I'd ever seen. His arm was around a child he was trying to shield from the Nazis who were whipping these poor souls trying to make them walk faster. All they could do was shuffle along and I saw one woman fall. The Nazi guard just pushed her out of the way with his boot. It seemed they were made to walk miles to the camp near the tunnels which they had begun to dig out.

When they were too ill to work they were pushed over the cliff, onto a small bay and lime was poured down there. There were hundreds pushed over the cliff but at the end of the war I don't think there was much left of them, they continually poured lime on and burned them. The only way we could find out about any of these things was from the locals who were forced labour.

My Mother was in the 'underground information' and from time to time the man who had worked in the tunnels, our neighbour, told her this particular group had been fed, allowed to sleep until the next day and then been made to work... all of them, men, women, and children. Whole families had arrived but they didn't last long, they had suffered so much, they had been starved and beaten and they died quickly. It seems no one knows where they put the bodies.

Those sights and those stories have stayed with me all my life... a nightmare which returns from time to time... I shudder when I think what must it have been like for those who were actually in the concentration and death camps?

I suppose I was about nine when all that happened but as I'm talking it seems like yesterday.

I was never allowed to go anywhere near the 'tunnels' as a child but I've been back since a number of times and I hate the place. Those walls just stink of death, despite what they have done to 'clean it up' and make it like an 'underground hospital'. It's not just the damp you can smell there, it's death, it's a horrible place with the most terrible atmosphere.

I think it was early in 1943 when German was made a compulsory language in schools. Systematically, since they had arrived, they had raided the libraries and schools and many books considered anti-Nazi or anti-German had been destroyed.

Down below in our big house after we had moved in we found in the big wash house two large tin baths full of books and comics and we read those comics all the war right through. They were threadbare by the time we had finished with them. I remember there were some Laurel and Hardy and things like that and I found some Rupert Books. A book I really treasured but lost during all the travelling over the years... was a large encyclopaedia. I read it and read it and read it. It had the full set of the tales of the Arabian Nights. During my life since it has been the only book in which I have found the entire set. It was my treasure. I suppose I was about 10 then, and I was reading about Greek mythology, which was also in the book.

We had been allowed to keep our piano and we also had a gramophone but that was confiscated because we were heard playing a recording of the 'Last Night of the Proms' which included 'God Save the King' and 'Land of Hope and Glory'. The Nazis heard this and took everything away.

The Germans didn't like you going to church. They didn't want you to have anything to hang on to, to have any faith. They wanted to break your morale first and foremost and then ill treat you afterwards and deprive you of things. They did everything possible to take away your dignity. Even as a child I could understand this, so I was as horrible as possible to them because to me a person's dignity should be left intact.

For the first couple of years mail used to come regularly then after that deliveries were only occasional. We heard that it was burned by the sackful and what we did get had been so heavily censored it was almost impossible to read it.

By the end of 1942 we were afraid to speak in public or in the long queues because some people had turned informers in order to get concessions and there were a number of women who would do anything to get silk stockings or chocolate or luxuries. Some of them lived with the Officers, but they were marked down by the 'underground information' group, in which my Mother was active so that at the end of the war the local people rounded up these women, took them to the Royal Square and attempted to tar and feather them. They were rescued by the British troops and put on the first boat to England.

By the end of 1944 we were almost starving and in the Autumn the gas supplies in Jersey ceased, then in January electricity ceased.

We had already become very weak and my brother and I no longer had the energy to go stealing or wandering on the docks. It was not until the end of 1944 the first Red Cross ship arrived. I remember it was called The Vega. We would have starved had it not come.

The Germans had broken into their own store houses but they were empty. They were eating acorns and I also was picking acorns. I saw some soldiers picking lumps of grass and eating it raw.

Whilst some of them were concerned only with finding something to eat others became increasingly aggressive, and we had to hide our domestic animals because we had heard they were taking them away to eat. More and more Russian prisoners were escaping and they too were looking for anything to eat. One Nazi Officer tried to confiscate my spaniel dog but I created such a fuss and screamed and screamed till he let it go.

Once the war ended, as soon as the liberation came, we were the only part of the British Isles where rationing was abolished. We could get anything we liked. Food and supplies were poured into the Island because of the deprivation of the war years. For the first two years after the liberation I remember my Grandmother giving me cod liver oil and malt, halibut liver oil and all the things that we'd needed. We had to take it gradually. Although the food was available a lot of it we couldn't eat except in very small quantities because our stomachs wouldn't take it, so it was a weaning process of two years to get us onto a proper diet and in the meantime she gave us all the vitamins and fish oils she could because we were scrawny little kids and we had some bone deformities. The joints looked huge and the rest of the legs were thin, there was no flesh.

It was during this time my Mother heard a rumour that if the situation got worse we would all be shot.

She said 'If it does come to that **I'm** going to do the shooting', and much to our surprise she produced a revolver. She said 'Rather than have **them** shoot you I'd rather we all died together'.

Turning to me she said 'I'll shoot you and your brother first, then your Grandma, then, turning to my Aunt and Uncle, 'you two and then myself'.

We were very afraid and all feeling very weak from want of food despite the Red Cross Parcels.

Then, thank God, came liberation day... that was wonderful but the food they offered us was no good because we were half starved and it gave us pains.

About a week after liberation my Mother, through her underground contacts, (it was still working), heard that days before our liberation, before the Germans had admitted defeat, a detail had arrived from Berlin that all civilians in the Channel Islands were to be called out to the Royal Square and the Churches and places like that in the belief that we would be read a proclamation but in fact the instructions were that everyone was to be machine gunned leaving not a single Channel Islander alive. But it was never acted upon because a revolt of the German soldiers was imminent. What a narrow escape we had! Do you wonder that May 9th is still held in such reverence by so many of us?

VASSILI MAREMPOLSKI'S STORY IN BRIEF

When the Germans invaded Russia and the Ukraine in 1941 Vassili was only 15. Together with a group of young men and girls of similar age they were bundled into lorries taken to the station and transported like cattle across Europe through Poland and into Germany, where the girls were sent to work. The young men continued across France to St. Malo and from there they were taken to Jersey where Vassili was made a Todt Worker.

Half starved, beaten the whole time, they were made to work 12 hours a day. Vassili escaped but was caught and badly beaten.

Vassili became weaker and weaker and fell ill with dysentery.

A Spanish Red Cross Worker befriended Vassili and he is convinced he was responsible for saving his life.

For a time Vassili was made to work on the excavations in the tunnels which is where he met Yegorka, who died.

Vassili fell ill again and this time his Spanish friend argued he was no longer fit for work. Eventually a German Medical Commission visited Immelman, the camp where Vassili was kept, and the Commission decided he and a number of his friends were no longer fit to work. Vassili believed he was being sent back to the Ukraine but is was more likely he was being sent to where most of the 'too weak to work prisoners' were being sent; to Neuengamme concentration camp, from whence they would be sent to gas-chambers.

On the short voyage from Jersey to France some of the boats were sunk by the British Navy. Vassili was saved and finished up in prison, in St. Malo. Again Vassili escaped. After many adventures he managed to work his way northwards and finally joined the Soviet Army in September 1944 in Eastern Germany.

VASSILI MAREMPOLSKI'S STORY OF WORKING IN THE 'GERMAN UNDERGROUND TUNNELS'

NOTE: *The 'mine' to which Vassili refers is in fact the 'tunnels'*

Once again the hard gloomy days of living in camp were dragging by. In a room filled with tobacco smoke, in cold and hunger, they seemed especially hard for me because I had already become used to normal food and hospital cleanliness. The camp policemen didn't miss any chance to torment those poor people, shadows, by forcing then to clean loos and the area in the camp and outside it.

One day I was called into the camp First Aid Ward. Going through the internal gates I noticed a familiar car with red crosses and my heart missed a beat with joyful anticipation. As I crossed the threshold of the ward I saw Mikhola Ivanovich who, together with a strange doctor in a white gown, was examining a skinny ill prisoner.

'Is that you, Marempolski? There's someone asking for you'

The person sitting at the table in another room and writing something turned out to be... the Spaniard.

'Vincente!' I exclaimed.

'Salute, pequeno*! Are you still alive?'

'As you see...'

We hugged each other vigorously.

'Well, how are things here in "Immelman"?'

'Like in jail. Awaiting to be sent off from the island but still we are here, yet. It's already Spring... And how are you doing?

'We are all right, fighting dysentery and typhus. Death-rate is high in Russian camps! It's a pity you're not with us. Senora Augusta was so worried when she learnt that you had been sent to the camp. She says 'hello' and sent you this parcel.'

'Thanks to you and to her... And what's new at the front?'

'Good news! The Red Army is on the offensive and pushing the Nazis back! It's liberated Kharkov.'

'Oh, the Ukraine is being liberated at last! Wonderful!'

At that moment the doctor came in and snapped to the Spaniard: 'Let's go!'

Vincente slipped the paper package into my hands and I swiftly hid it under the flap of my jacket.

'God bless you!'

'Say 'hello' to all the comrades, Vincente!'

The car pulled out.

'Well, are you happy to have met him' Slavin asked.

'Sure, I am. This Spaniard saved my life.'

'And what's the news... at the front?'

'Our troops beat the hell out of Germans! Kharkov is liberated.

'Good news! Tell that to lads...'

I shared the bread and cheese contained in the parcel with Grisha and a few other hungry comrades who were very pleased with the present.

Who's giving away the loaves here?' Mustafa was trying to find out. 'What kind of chap is doing that? So share some with me!'

But Mustafa didn't get a crumb...

The following day the camp Commandant Fritz Budrich saw some people hanging around the camp square in broad daylight. He ordered to fall in all the inhabitants of the 'ward of loafers'.

'You eat the bread for nothing here while I am short of men for work!' he declared through the interpreter Mr Novak. He walked in front of the ranks of cripples pointing his finger at those who appeared fit to him and ordered them to take three steps forward. There turned out to be about a dozen such men : I and Grisha Borodily among them.

'Tomorrow everyone of you must turn up to your chief's column and go arbeit*. To work! And don't try to idle, loafers, or you'll be beaten up.'

Mr Novak put everyone down on his list and warned that our names would be submitted to the chief by the evening.

'That's the way we are sent off the island!' I said to Grisha bitterly.

Once again the past events repeated. In the morning Black blew his police whistle, the sound of which I never forgot. I rushed out of the 'ward of loafers' and joined the column. Grisha followed me running. Even in the dark I noticed quite a few unfamiliar faces. Black counted the men, then pulled out a paper from his pocket and yelled; 'Marempolski, Borodi, are they here?'

'Yes we're here.'

'Move up, loafers!'

The column crossed the gates of 'Immelman' and turned in the direction of the railway.

'Where are they taking us? Where are we going to work?' I asked Vassili Dusheikho who was next to me.

'Don't you know? To the mine... We've been working underground for nearly two weeks already.'

'And who are those new men in our brigade?'

'They sent reinforcements from "Udet". Our column had lost half of its men.... Max disposed of them: some were beaten to death, others are sick...

'Well, I see. I wondered who those strange lads in our column were!'

'They brought two hundred of them recently and divided them between the brigades.'

'So Mikhail Melnik might be here too. He is from my village Markushi.'

'I don't know him but if you look closely you may recognise him.'

When the dawn broke, and the men of the column weren't walking in ranks any longer, I started looking closely at them. They were mainly young lads: skinny, exhausted, in ragged and patched clothes, blue from cold and some of them were swollen from starvation. There was no Mikhail Melnik among them. Then I noticed a few familiar faces among newcomers, probably, those fellow-countrymen with whom I was brought by train. However, I didn't recognise at once who they were, except for one short guy.

'You're Mikhola Ostapchuk, aren't you, my friend?' I asked a thoughtful lad of my own age, who, probably, at that very moment was thinking about a delicious meal in his homeland. The lad startled as if he was stung.

'Yes I am... And who are you? Oh, hang on, you're Vassili from Markushi.'

'That's right. I'm Vassili Marempolski.'

'How come you're here?'

'I was sent back to my column after hospital. Have you been here long?'

'We were sent from "Udet" to reinforce your "Immelman" just two weeks ago.'

'So where is better: Here or there?'

'It's damned the same everywhere! There, it was German Schefer who was finishing us off, here it's Max Black. Both are worthy of each other.

'What are you doing in "Udet"?'

'Everything Germans ordered: digging trenches for cables, holes for pill-boxes, then filling them with concrete. It was damned hard. The only thing I remember is clanking of pickaxes and spades and the peculiar sound of prisoners' wooden stocks, the endless angry barking and swearing in German of overseers beating us with truncheons and hoses...'

'What are we in for? Do you know when they are going to send us off from here?'

'There was a lot of talks about it, but, obviously, no bee can slip out of this swarm! There's no way out, my friend. Probably, we'll have to lay our bones on this island! No strength left any more... And where did you happen to be?'

'I worked in Black's column all the time, then caught dysentery and was taken to hospital.... I hardly survived. Spaniards saved my life.'

'Well in "Udet" Spaniards are separated from us by barbed wire fence. They cherish us, Russians, so much and help us as well as they can.

'And did you go AWOL?'

'We do it all the time, nobody is afraid for his life. How many times we used our chance to carry out, I would say, cheeky outings from the camp at night. Though that's not so simple: you put your life at stake. But hunger drives us forward: beetroot, swede, potato are behind the fence. Maybe that's why I'm alive.'

'Mikola, what kind of mine are we now going to? Is it coal extracted there or iron ore?'

'Nothing of the kind! It's just underground, galleries. We dig them in length rather than in depth. Probably, they'll become bunkers for Germans to hide from English bombs. You're going to see yourself.

At that moment Black's command resounded: 'Move up! Fall into rank of fours!'

We seemed to approach that mine. First, we walked through the hills, then descended into a deep valley surrounded by a barbed wire fence with frequent posts with warning 'Mines!' in three languages: German, English, and even Russian. On the top of the hill there were a few English houses with pigs grazing near one of them and the apple-tree grove all around, but downhill, on this side of the fence : the gates with SS guards armed with sub-machine guns and Alsatians. As we were going through the gates, the Alsatians were straining at the leash. When we crossed a small clearing a wide entrance of the gallery opened in front of us. It looked like a huge hole. The very sight of the underground gave me the creeps. We weren't going down but were walking along a lengthy corridor hollowed in granite. Electric lights lit damp walls with protuberant sharp rocks. On both sides of the main corridor there were other, smaller ones. It was a real stone labyrinth underground. In some places the timbering supported high vaults. Water was dripping here and there.

The black depth smelled with grave chill. The traces from pickaxe blows were stamped on the shapeless walls. Mud floundered under the feet : soil and barren rock mixed with underground waters. In the main-corridor and in the labyrinth of smaller ones, everywhere, people were stirring like grey little ants. Pickaxes hammering, shouting and yelling, mud floundering under the feet... It was hard to believe that all the underground was hollowed in no time by the hands of exhausted, starved Russian prisoners. There was only one way out for those who broke down : death.

Our brigade with Max Heinz-Black in charge worked in a remote corridor of the underground labyrinth. A dynamite explosion had been carried out there on night shift and then we were crushing, crushing large rocks into tiny pieces with pickaxes, shovelling them into trolleys to be pushed along the tracks to the exit by a couple of lads. Then the rocks were dumped into a ravine. In a word, the work was similar to the one we had done on the railway embankment with the only difference of it being done in the mine.

On top of that, most of the prisoners were extremely weakened and were unable to lift a shovel with rocks to throw them into a trolley. Black kept urging the lads. I happened to work together with one fellow-countryman, also a former PoW, Ivan Adamchuk from the village of Lipyatino. And that's the way we did it : I was holding a shovel filled with rocks and Ivan was pulling at a rope tied to its handle and by joint efforts we managed to dump the rocks into a trolley.

That was going on throughout weeks which turned into months. The work was extremely difficult : we were hollowing a tunnel through a solid virgin crag. Hundreds of thousands of tons of rock we extracted from there. The prisoners from 'Immelman', as well as from concentration camps 'Schepke' and 'Udet' were working underground the whole 24 hours, in two 12 hour shifts. Though, our fourth brigade was working only in the first shift. There were numerous casualties, especially from explosions and blasts. The prisoners who worked inside the crag were given something resembling broken miners' helmets but they didn't protect them from injuries. Quite a few prisoners were injured by splinters of flying rocks, some were deafened. After a few days of underground explosions I became deaf in my right ear. Those severely injured were taken by SS guards elsewhere and no one has ever seen them again.

A few deaths of Russian prisoners happened before my eyes. Once our brigade came to work in the morning when a landslip had happened in the adjacent tunnel and three men had been killed. The prisoners from 'Schepke' dug the bodies out, rolled them in tarpaulin and loaded them on a truck. What happened to their bodies is unknown. There was s rumour that many dead bodies were dumped into the ocean from a cliff and then they floated away from the shore. *(See elsewhere for a similar story)*.

In a week eighteen Soviet prisoners lost their lives under a landslide. As Germans said afterwards, they were buried in a communal grave at the cemetery Saint-Saviore. Nobody knows exactly how many prisoners have died in those tunnels...

Nowadays they accommodate the museum of German Occupation of the island of Jersey. **Incidentally, there was a view that the Nazis had intended to build a gas chamber for extermination of weak and mentally handicapped people as well as their political opponents. *****

The Occupation of Jersey is known to have begun on the 1st of July 1940. The work on construction of the tunnel started in the summer of 1942 and continued for nearly two years. Originally, it was planned to use the tunnel as an ordnance depot. **In 1944 it was converted into a hospital** and came into service after D day (the allied troops landing in Normandy). Great numbers of wounded German soldiers and Officers fled the French coast for Jersey and found shelter in its secure walls. The construction of the hospital wasn't completed regardless of the fact that 14,000 tons of barren rock had been extracted and 4,000 tons of reinforced concrete structures had been installed. The floor area of the tunnel accounted for 2,265 square metres.

Italian Officer Realini is now known to have been the senior architect of the underground complex. Organisation of Todt* was responsible for the implementation of the project and a certain Major Tishman, an elderly man of about 65 years old, was civil engineer. Before the war he had worked for nearly 20 years as civil engineer in Africa.

Nowadays, the tunnels accommodate the museum of the German Occupation of the island of Jersey. The former prisoner of the Jersey camp, the member of the anti-fascist Resistance, Joe Miere, was in charge of the museum, until recently.

Days, weeks, months of exhausting labour in the mine went by. The fourth brigade of Max Heinz, nicknamed Black, pushed itself a few dozen metres forward in the underground gallery. Once after a short lunch break I was hammering with my pickaxe against an overhanging rock when suddenly before I even realised, the rock broke loose from the wall and crashed next to me, catching my right foot. I collapsed, blood gushing out of my crushed foot as sheer pain overwhelmed me.

'What's wrong? Are you all right, Vassili?' Grisha leapt towards me.

'I don't know... I am a cripple now...'

Black ran up and shouted something in German.

'The rock fell down on the comrade.'

Instead of sympathising with the poor prisoner Black burst out with outrageous German abuse : 'You, loafers, don't want to work and do your best not to turn up at work, Fierfluchter gund!'

Unable to get up I had lain on a stony surface until the evening before, leaping on one foot, I was taken under my arms to the camp. I lay about for a week in the camp First Aid ward and then, when I could walk with a stick, I was transferred to the 'ward of loafers' again.

Again the winter fog spread behind the windows; it was raining and the ocean was roaring fiercely. Thoughts were racing in my mind : when will freedom and liberation come, when I shall be taken back from this island to my native Ukraine...? ** see 'Yegorka's story'

ADDENDUM TO VASSILI MAREMPOLSKI'S STORY ABOUT THE UNDERGROUND HOSPITAL

Yegorka's Story

Following the translation from the Ukrainian of Chapter XIV, the Author, (with the help of the interpreter) questioned Vassili Marempolski about the suggestion that the 'underground hospital' (it was simply called 'the tunnels' then) was intended as a gas chamber eventually and could have been easily converted for such a purpose.

It transpired that amongst those who had been prisoners in Borkum Camp on Alderney was a Russian Jew of the name Yegorka who, for some unknown reason with a few others... possibly because they were fitter than most and therefore suitable for work on the Channel Islands fortifications, had been taken from Birkenau (the overflow extermination camp to Auschwitz) and sent to Alderney.

This is Vassili's story...

"I met Yegorka in the tunnels where I had been working for days. I had been forced to dig and dig and dig until the blisters on my hands bled and the spade slipped in my hands with the blood.

I had never met an Alderney prisoner before. Usually the Nazi soldiers and the SS kept us separated. It seemed that the Ukrainians and the Spanish were kept in Jersey and the Russians and the Jews sent to Alderney. Yegorka was working near me. I spoke to him and as I did so he cringed. He did not look up. Simply bent his head lower like a cowed dog.

He was stooped like an old man but he could not have been any older than me and I was only 16. His skin was stretched tight over his face and hands and his bones protruded. He was terribly thin. He was like a walking skeleton, his cheeks hollow and his skin a dirty yellow colour. His head was shaved.

He was wearing the pyjamas all prisoners were forced to wear. When he realised I was friendly he edged nearer but seemed only half aware, a man in a semi-coma of hunger and fatigue. He seemed hardly able to lift the spade.

He looked at me with glazed, sightless eyes yet I knew he wanted to speak, to tell me something.

He mumbled something and I knew he was Russian but I understood he had said 'keep away'. As he spoke he coughed and a little speck of blood appeared on his lips.

He made no effort to wipe it away – I don't think he knew it was there.

He had no shoes or boots – his feet were covered in rags. He scratched and looked at me trying to convey he was covered in lice, it seemed. He glanced fearfully over his shoulder, terrified of the SS guard who repeatedly beat us with their truncheons. It seemed the Alderney prisoners received the worst treatment. It seemed the SS and the guards were doing everything possible to accelerate the deaths of many.

My morsel of biscuit which he accepted without smile or acknowledgement he put slowly between his lips, his jaw moving to masticate in slow motion, only brought on another coughing spasm and more blood.

I felt guilty. So far as he was able he demonstrated his gratefulness. He tried to speak. His words were simple, staccato. It was impossible under the watchful eye of the guards to hold a conversation but during the two or three days we worked together I learned that he had been transferred from Birkenau to Alderney.

He said he had been forced to carry corpses from the gas chambers to the incinerators. That was how he had stayed alive. He said even the work in the tunnels, which was soon to kill him he knew, was preferable to what had been forced upon him in Birkenau.

Yegorka tried to explain that the shape and size of the tunnels were like those in Birkenau. He told me he was sure they were going to be used as gas chambers and warned me that eventually, I too, would be forced to do similar work when the Nazis won the war.

I did my best to help him but the guards watched us all the time. One day Yegorka did not arrive. I looked for him each day but I never saw him again. I'm sure he died. He never again appeared to work in the tunnels.

A CONVERSATION WITH MR. JOE MIERE
Custodian of the underground hospital in Jersey for many years.

Note: Mr. Miere can be proud of his success in being largely responsible for building up over the years the fine, interesting displays and records to be seen in the underground hospital.

Whilst Mr. Miere can trace his ancestry back to good Norman and Breton stock with pride, but he is never the less a loyal Channel Islander. Born in St. Helier, Jersey on the 27th July 1926 he was 14 at the time of the Occupation and living in a house about one mile inland on the outskirts of town. Educated in the Roman Catholic De La Salle College he quickly became aware of what it was like to live under the heel of an invading army.

One day Joe Miere read in the Jersey Evening Post, in July 1940, of an Irishman in civilian clothes who had once been an Irish Guardsman, sitting in a cafe. A German soldier walked in and told the Irishman to take off his hat in the presence of a German soldier. The Irishman took no notice. The soldier again demanded. The Irishman refused, so the soldier knocked his hat off, at which the Irishman hit the soldier.

Very quickly the Irishman was arrested and received a 6 month sentence from the Jersey Magistrate who was keen not to stir up too much trouble with the German Authorities.

All this happened in the early days of the Occupation and it was a lesson which Joe Miere wisely remembered. In those days many of the Germans believed they were already in England and that the war would be over in 6 months.

ᘓᘔ

The Author: Joe, do you think you were perhaps encouraged by that story of the Irishman?

Joe: Well, yes, perhaps I was. There was a group of us, perhaps a dozen. We became involved in minor acts of 'resistance'. Just 'pin-pricks' to irritate and annoy the Germans. some of them became involved in printing and distributing leaflets. That was a much more serious crime. I did not, but I **was** arrested on 16th September 1942 when I was one of a large crowd of Islanders protesting at St. Helier harbour.

The Germans were deporting some 2200 English and U.K. born Channel Islanders to internment camps in Germany.

We did what we could to obstruct them because we thought it was wrong, they had committed no crimes, they were simply not 'Jersey born'. Many of us were arrested by armed German soldiers. We were put in prison in St. Helier and kept there overnight. Next day we were interrogated, then released with a warning that if we protested again we would be sent to Germany too, if we did anything against the German forces.

But as the days went on, every time the Germans organised more deportations of the English people we protested again, but this time we were not caught. But some others were and they were put in prison. A friend of mine was sent to a concentration camp. He was there for three years. He came back to Jersey when the war ended but he was a broken man. He died in 1974. He never really recovered. He came from a French family. No one seems to remember him. His name was Emile Barbier. Even after all these years I feel upset telling you about him. I wish the Island and the English would honour his memory as we honour him even after death.

The Author: You feel very strongly about these things Joe... even after all this time...

Joe Miere: Yes I do. Only those who have experienced these things would, I think, really understand. There was another occasion when I ran into trouble.

I was about to take communion when I noticed the shape and colour of the priests shoes. I realised he was a German Army Chaplain. I can even remember the time of day. It was 9am in the morning. He was serving mass at St. Thomas' R.C. church. When I realised who and what the Priest was I refused to take communion from him, but the Roman Catholic

French Priest intervened. He said 'This German Chaplain is a good man'. I said 'A good Priest cannot serve God and the devil Hitler at the same time'. Father Marie said the German Priest would be shot if he openly turned against Hitler, so I said 'Well, Father, the German Chaplain's boss Jesus died for his faith, why cannot the German Chaplain do the same and prove that he is a real Roman Catholic Priest?'

I can still see Father Marie's face as he turned and walked away without saying another word. He knew there was no answer to that.

The Author: That was brave of you Joe.

Joe Miere: I don't know about that... we all have our convictions even when we are hungry. Do you know there were some farmers who secretly helped the Germans and gave them extra food? They knew we were short of food but they were afraid. Other farmers helped the Islanders though.

Do you know a quarter pound of tea on the black market would cost at least £8? Later on it rose to £25.

Dried grated potatoes, turned into a powder were used as a blancmange substitute. Then there was carrot tea, and acorn coffee. The most dangerous of all was a distillation of 'cider' which we turned into a rough 'Calvados' (a kind of brandy). It was pure firewater. A drink of that and you were drunk for two days. We used to call it 'rocket fuel'!

Did you know we messed about with cherry leaves to make a tobacco substitute?

We were very, very hungry. Nearing the end of the Occupation people were almost starving. The German Army had already taken all the household pets. We were reduced to catching seagulls and sparrows. We soon found the seagulls were uneatable. Too tough. The sparrows were eatable but so small they provided little substance. The seagulls were all covered in lice.

You know, I think the real heroes of the Occupation were the mothers who gave up their own meagre rations for the sake of their children. I sometimes wonder how they stayed alive.

The Author: Joe, I've heard there were a lot of informers... is that true?

Joe Miere: I wouldn't have said there 'were a lot'. There were enough of them to make one careful what one said in public. I think some were merely settling old scores dating back before the Occupation. Women did, just to get chocolate or stockings. Others informed just to get extra food. The Germans used them but I'm sure they didn't respect them.

The Author: You once told me you had become a hairdresser.

Joe Miere: Yes I did. The Germans began to use forced labour. I could see the conditions were little better than for the imported prisoners, By becoming a hairdresser I avoided mobilisation.

Conditions got worse and worse as the years wore on. The Germans brought in Secret Field Police and large numbers of young Nazi soldiers and with them the relationship between the population and occupying forces deteriorated.

There was about a dozen of us I suppose. Some of my group tried to identify the collaborators – or those they thought were collaborating – by painting swastikas on their houses.

That got us into real trouble. And **me** into trouble. It was 1944 and by the time the German Secret Field Police **and** the German Naval Police were after me. Some Good Friends of mine gave me a safe place to hide whilst the Germans searched my house. It took them quite a time because there were 19 rooms. My family didn't have time to clear my room so the Germans found some British leaflets (you know the British used to drop leaflets from time to time on the Islands to cheer us up)... and, what was worse, some 9mm German ammunition.

When they couldn't find me they sent a message to my sister to say that if I didn't give myself up they would arrest my entire family. They gave me 48 hours to give myself up. I couldn't let that happen to my family so I went round to the Field Police Headquarters.

They started beating me up almost straight away when I wouldn't answer their questions. It went on for night after night. They knocked my front teeth out. In the end I couldn't feel anything – I just hurt all over and I'd closed my mind to it all.

In the end they gave up trying to make me speak, so they put me before a Military Court. They sentenced me to 2 years. Later they reduced it to eighteen months.

The Author: Why did they do that?

Joe Miere: Strange really. I couldn't make out how their minds worked. They said it was because although they found ammo they found no guns or arms. They moved me away from Field Police Headquarters to another prison where the German guards were not so brutal.

I got into trouble there too because I refused to stand when the prison Kommandant came into my cell. I was in solitary confinement for that.

The Author: What were your feelings about that?

Joe Miere: I suppose by fighting back I maintained my morale, even when I was in solitary. It was a good thing I did not know that whilst I was in prison they had arrested my Grandfather, my Father and one of my sisters. Not all at the same time. I think they were trying to find out what I had refused to tell them. But my family couldn't tell because I had never told them. What not one of us had told the Germans was that my two brothers were serving in the British Army.

The Author: You must be very proud of your family Joe.

Joe Miere: Yes I am... very proud indeed. We are a loyal family. Loyal to one another. Loyal to Jersey and loyal to Britain.

I joined the British Army a few days after liberation day. I wanted to fight the Japs.

The Author: That's where I was Joe. I'd been out there for five years.

Joe Miere: Well, they wouldn't take me for that. I got posted to Germany and I was demobed in 1948.

It wasn't until I got to Germany I realised what devastation our bombing had caused. It was a terrible mess. The children and the old folks were suffering as we had done in the Islands during the last year of the Occupation. We used to feed the little German children and give food parcels to the old folk. That was what some of the older Germans soldiers had done for us. It was a sort of return.

The Author: One hears rumours Joe of prisoners being buried in concrete as the fortifications were being built because they could no longer work. Is that true?

Joe Miere: There is a story of a prisoner who accidentally fell into concrete as they were building an anti-tank sea wall at St. Ouens Bay. The Germans tried to get him out but failed. Even that rumour had never been confirmed and as for the rest I doubt it, but how would I know? I was in prison some of the time.

The Author: That is so. But you didn't know what was going on in Guernsey or Alderney or for that matter in some parts of this Island.

Joe Miere: That is true.

The Author: Joe... you have said you are loyal to Britain yet you have on more than one occasion expressed resentment against the British Government during the war for failing to feed the Channel Islanders when they were feeding the Greeks.

Joe Miere: That is true – I have. I would like to know why it happened.

The Channel Islands are very small indeed and what they have contributed towards Britain during two world wars is out of all proportion to their size.

In the 1914-18 war 12,000 Channel Islanders served with the loss of 2200 killed and in 1939-45 10,000 Channel Islanders from all over the world served in the Forces with 600 dead.

On top of this during the war the British Government did a number of silly things which made matters worse for us here. In 1945 we were starving. If the Red Cross had not arrived in

December 1944 many of us would have starved to death by May 1945.

I think there are a lot of questions still to be answered. The secret files should have been released when the war ended. The people of Jersey wanted an inquiry and investigation into war time collaboration in Jersey, but twice the Jersey Authorities turned down the request. The people who had turned it down were the same ones who had been in office during the war. I think that speaks for itself.

No wonder the British press and other people are always trying to get at the truth. Something smells.

The Author: I am personally grateful for your outspoken comments and I'm sure people who read what you have said will be equally grateful and interested.

TOMMY SYMS TESTIMONY

This is the story of Tommy Syms.

It is the story of a very young boy, deprived of proper schooling, hungry all the time, and who, at the age of ten with his father and mother, was transported to a German concentration camp.

Tom told his story on February 5th 1995. The restraint in his narration and the laconic terms in which he described what must have been a bewildering, endless and frightening series of experiences for a boy of that age can only be admired.

Tommy Syms way of telling is not unlike that of the Ukrainian prisoner Vassili Marempolski. As with so very many survivors from the concentration camps it had taken all of the forty years from those dark days for the victims to be able to talk about their experiences. From time to time there is a strange numbness in the manner of telling as if the narrator were speaking of someone else or as if it was merely the memory of a dream.

Born in 1932 he was only eight when the German jackboots thundered through the streets of St. Helier, Jersey and, like Margaret James (Brockley) who was only six at the time, for him there was the same mixture of fear, no doubt acquired through the reactions of his parents, and of curiosity because he was quite unaware of the meaning of the presence of these impressive soldiers.

Tommy's father had arrived in 1930 from Cornwall seeking work. He found work. He also found a lovely Jersey girl named Eva Maud Minier. Within a year they had married and in due course Tommy was born. Tommy proved to be their only child.

His life before the Occupation was one of uncaring, happy days when the sun seemed always to be shining and his parents always smiling.

Then, without warning and quite suddenly, everything changed. All kinds of strange stories were exchanged between the children at his school. The relaxed and happy atmosphere of his home became one of tension and whispered consultations between his Mother and Father. they asked him what were his favourite toys and which of his warm clothes he liked best, because they were all going on a boat trip, and he would not be able to take many things. Then one day his Grandfather arrived and he watched his parents packing some of the nice things in their home on to a trolley. He asked 'Aren't we coming back mum?' and his Mother 'Yes, your Grandpa is looking after these for us whilst we are away'. 'When are we going mum?', and she replied 'Tomorrow darling'.

The following day, carrying a suitcase each, they walked down to the quay. Tommy was surprised to see hundreds of other people, all carrying suitcases, and amongst whom were some of his school pals. Everyone was hurrying and some were pushing their way through urging their lagging, bewildered children.

The quay was already crowded when they arrived and people were talking, some were shouting and many of the women were crying as they said 'good bye' to friends and relations. They were formed into a jostling queue of people, many standing on tip-toe straining to see how far it was to the gangplank up which people were struggling to the ship.

The ship was already crowded. Every deck, every spot on which someone could sit or stand was already occupied. Many were waving or calling out to people they knew still waiting in the queue.

Then, without warning, a man on the ship's bridge shouted to the policeman controlling the people going on to the gangplank. Other men began releasing the ships hawsers, the ship's hooter sounded and the gangplank was withdrawn.

Immediately cries of protest from the crowds left standing on the quay arose. There were scuffles and the atmosphere of panic and despair in which Tommy found himself was one he never forgot. He remembers the overloaded boat which had waited until the last minute, pulling away and the great ropes vanishing through the hawse-holes in the ship's bows. Without knowing why he absorbed the feelings of despair and disappointment from those around him finally they turned and trudged back to their house, his parents arguing hotly.

The following day he heard his father telling his mother that there had been other ships waiting to come into the harbour to take more people away but they had been turned back empty.

Tom has always been convinced that this was true. That the Jersey Authorities decided there was no need for panic and all would be well for those who stayed behind.

It has since been admitted by Whitehall that the whole population of the Channel Islands could have been evacuated before the Germans arrived.

Tommy later learned, that his parents could not decide whether to keep him with them or let him go alone with hundreds of other children.

The day Tommy had seen the ship leave the harbour was 20th June. Eight days later Heinkels swept across the Islands straffing and bombing the three main towns and ports. On July 1st Tommy saw people picking up leaflets which had been dropped by German airplanes.

Soon his mother was searching in cupboards for something white to hang from the window. 'What's that for mummy?' and his mother replied grimly 'The Germans are coming darling... there's nothing to be afraid of' and she hugged him closely.

Rightly of wrongly Tommy Syms blames Bailiff A.M. Coutanche for what happened to him from there on. He is very bitter about this.

The Syms' had lived in Maufaunt in a two roomed cottage in St. Saviour and his school was only hundreds of yards away.

Almost immediately on the arrival of the Germans the Syms' decided to move next door to Minier's Father, who had a smallholding. The move was not difficult for there was only a small amount of furniture and belongings, and this was put on a cart loaned by a farmer.

This second home called 'Valetta' wasn't much bigger than the one they had left but it had the advantage of offering the opportunity to keep a few chickens, and Eva's Father was some sort of protection for her in the absence of her husband who was away all day working.

What was to prove a greater advantage later was the ability to hide a radio in the area which lay between the two houses. The Germans, with all their searching, never found it in the two years leading up to the day orders were issued that all English born people were to be deported.

The intervening two years between Occupation and being told to leave the Island were little use to Tommy educationally for the Germans immediately took over St. Peters, his local school, as a temporary barracks and in the process of doing so destroyed all the books and papers and most of the equipment.

From then on the children were obliged to use a large old house as a makeshift school with little or no equipment, paper, pencils or books. The house was called 'Beaconsfield' on Old Beaumont Hill.

It was ironic that whilst the Germans made no effort to provide the educational needs of the school they demanded, in 1942, that German should become a compulsory language taught.

Within 3 months of arrival the German Commandant of the Occupying Forces had issued orders that all British males between the ages of 18 to 35 must register. This included Eva's husband and, if the Occupation lasted long enough, his Mother realised, would also include her son.

At the same time, a separate edict appeared in the *'Jersey Evening Post* 'that all Jews must be registered and included many more demands.

Such a prospect, to a Mother of an only son, could only fill her with anxiety and fear for the future, for Tommy's parents had an additional, personal fear, of which Tommy could not be aware.

Because of a whim Tommy's parents had had him circumcised. Mr Syms, a Cornishman, was not a Jew nor was his wife Eva who came from a long line of Jersey families of Breton stock.

Since the arrival of the Germans the parents of children in the Islands were constantly exhorting their children not to speak to or upset the Germans for fear of some sort of reprisal or punishment.

Because of their secret fear following the edict about the Jews, Tommy's parents were constantly cautioning him and admonishing him to the point of tears, without any logical explanation. So far as he was concerned they were being unfair and unreasonable.

One forgetful moment and Tommy might be seen by a German to be circumcised and that could lead to a situation too fearsome to contemplate. In the hands of an indifferent and vindictive German administrator not prepared to listen, Tommy could be labelled a Jew and through him, his parents, and they would all be sent away for extermination to one of the concentration camps.

The one document which could prove that Tommy's parents were not Jewish and that he had been born on the Island and that, although circumcised, he was not Jewish, was his birth certificate.

At all costs it was imperative that Tommy should retain this document, and that he should never be without it.

It is some measure of the mental strain and pressure which the necessity never to lose it had become part of his life that to this day he should have it with him when interviewed by the Author. It had become the sine qua non of his life.

One day Tommy, who had learned the art of stealing from the Germans and yet managed to avoid being caught, came home to find a distraught Mother.

Troops had arrived and were in the process of upending all the furniture, tearing pictures off the walls, upsetting the beds and even tearing part of the staircase to pieces, all in an effort to find a radio. They never found it.

Two days later his parents received a notice instructing them to be ready to leave the Island in the next 24 hours. The only luggage permitted was a small suitcase each. Tommy had vivid memories of having done this once before. It was September 17th 1942 and Tommy was ten.

They were not told why they were leaving nor where they were going. In fact, there was no information available and it became apparent only later on that a list had been prepared the previous year by the Island authorities on the demand of the German Command as part of a move to register everyone on the Island with a view of issuing identity cards with photographs.

Allegations have since been made that the Jersey Authorities had prepared a list of English born residents between September 1939 and the arrival of the Nazis in July 1940.

Whether this is true or not Tommy's deportation to a concentration camp at the age of ten was a direct result of being on that list.

It seems unlikely that the Syms family could have avoided deportation, and so Tommy once more found himself in a queue of people, having packed his suitcase, waiting to board a ship for St. Malo.

Alongside of them were Mr and Mrs Dunkley. Tommy remembers their name because he heard the Dunkleys telling his Mother and Father they had come to the Islands on holiday and been unable to get away. They too were to spend three years in Biberach.

There were a number of small ships making the passage all packed with men, women and children, the women and children being sent into the hold.

Either side of the transportation ships were German vessels packed with troops and Tommy tells of the journey, which was conducted at night, being enlivened by the singing of the troops and all the lights ablaze on the ships.

Almost immediately Tommy found himself being bundled aboard a train consisting of dozens of cattle trucks and a few carriages with hard seats. The journey for Tommy seemed never ending with only occasional stops for the distribution of scanty bits of food and to meet the needs of nature. Dorsten, a transit camp on the Emms canal near Dortmund, some 500 miles, from St. Malo, was the destination.

It was a nightmare journey made worse when the train was stopped, the doors of the truck flung back and a menacing soldier waved a rifle indicating to Tommy's Father that he must dismount. Tommy and his distraught Mother saw him being marched away with a lot of other men.

Eventually they arrived in Dorsten. There were no proper facilities and families slept on the floor, covered in straw, in a big hall. They were there three months and would have starved had it not been for the scraps of food given them secretly by inmates of a nearby PoW camp.

After another miserable and anxious journey, not knowing what had happened to his father, Tommy and his Mother arrived at Biberach concentration camp.

The feelings of Tommy and his Mother have to be imagined; having seen his father taken away, he and his Mother were now separated, he being sent to a barrack room for children over ten and his Mother to barrack room No. 5.

In Tommy's own words this is what happened to him in Biberach.

'When we first arrived it was being run by the SS. It had previously been a PoW camp. Then quite soon we heard that the SS were being sent to the Russian front and a group called the Volk Sturn (rather like our Home Guard) were brought in to run the camp.

Things improved from then on and the camp began to be better organised. I was able to see my mother and spend time with her and Red Cross food parcels began to arrive. We were lucky to get these because under the Geneva Convention only PoWs were entitled to Red Cross parcels.

We were not ill treated like the Jews but there was always the thought that anything might happen. In the winter of 1944 the Germans said more inmates were coming into Biberach and they wanted volunteers to help them.

We were told to go to Biberach railway station sidings where a train shunted in. It consisted of cattle waggons. When the doors were flung back nobody got out.

Some crawled to the doors and fell out, a few were helped out by us but a lot remained where they were... they were all dead, I think there were about 200 of them, and the train had come from Belsen. We didn't know why they were sent to Biberach. We heard they were American Jews but what difference that made we didn't know.

It sent a shiver round the camp because we had already heard of the horrors in the other camps and the gassings and we all thought by bringing Jews into Biberach that we too were for the gaschambers.

Then sometime in 1943, a wonderful thing happened – my Father arrived and was put into barrack room No. 6. When we were separated he had been taken to Laufen for some reason and now he was back with us.

Food was very short and at times we were half starved or worse, saved only by food parcels. The Jews were separated from us. They were in a terrible state and deaths occurred daily.

We never found out why we had been deported. We had not been told when we left Jersey and we never found out from the letters which eventually began to arrive. We got no message from Coutanche.

When we had arrived in Dorsten my Mother and I were vaccinated but we didn't know what it was for and we were very frightened. We thought we were to be killed. It was strange but my Mother and I seemed to keep pretty well but there were a lot of young people who died of meningitis and TB. There was a nice couple, a Mr and Mrs Waring with a 2 year old boy named Rex. I used to push him around in an old perambulator, just for something to do, but he too died of meningitis.

I think there must have been over a thousand of us in the camp. My number was 478 and my Mother's 479. We were not tattooed. My Father's number was 1259.

Biberach had originally been a camp for British Officer PoWs and was called Oflag 55. It was a fairly easy camp from which to escape and when occupied by them many tunnelled out beyond the barbed wire fencing. The Germans knew they were going to escape and waited for them to come out. The whole lot were mown down with machine guns with the exception of one who escaped to Switzerland.

I remember that soon after arriving in Biberach all the unattached women were sent to another camp called Liebenau. I don't know what happened to them. There was a lot of speculation. I remember one very beautiful girl with red hair called Betty Brandon. Then there was Hazel Guy, who was only 15 when we left Jersey. I remember her parents Mary and William, they were nice people.

My Mother was only 30 when the Germans walked in. Like a lot of people who were interned in the camps she died very young, aged 47. It was the condition, the poor food, and the awful strain.

We used to watch the Hitler Youth training for the front up on the hill beyond Biberach. They never came near the camp. We young ones seemed to find things to do but the adults must have been terribly bored. Many of the Mothers gave their meagre rations to their children, which is perhaps why my Mother died.

Camp rations were very poor. We used to get a watery soup with bits of root vegetable floating in it. The tea was dreadful. They called it 'lime' tea. The food parcels from all over the world kept us going.

Then on April 23rd 1945 we were liberated.

The French arrived first. It was the 4th Battalion of Moroccan shocktroops. Then a bit later the Americans arrived and took over. They had wonderful food but some of the inmates couldn't eat it. It was too rich and they were ill. everyone wanted to rush out of the gates but there was nowhere to go and in the end we were there for six weeks.

We left a lot of Jews, Greeks and Benghazi's there. I don't know what happened to them.

Whilst we were waiting two French nurses were shot by a 14 year old German boy. They caught him and executed him on the spot.

When the troops heard of the murder of the French nurses they rounded up some Germans put them in a barn, put their guns through the windows and shot them all.

The Americans moved in to stop them and there was a dangerous moment when the Moroccan troops and the Americans faced one another.

Eventually, said Tommy, the British arrived and took us out.

We were taken to Mengen airfield where we were flown to Hendon Airport. We were all supposed to have somewhere to go. There was no one there to help us and what happened to those who knew no one in England I don't know. We were lucky because we had relations in Chepstow where we stayed for six weeks whilst we waited for permission to go back to Jersey. I think they were removing all the Germans and bringing them back to England to put into PoW camps.

When we did get back almost all the furniture in our house had gone and someone else was living there. We had only rented it and whilst we'd been away someone else had moved in.

There was, I remember a lot of talk about a man called James Lingshaw who had reported his Mother to the Germans for helping Russian prisoners. She was sent to a concentration camp where she died.

I remember my Father talking about Lingshaw because he had been amongst those deported from Jersey and was with my Father in Laufen.

Because of what he had done to help the Germans he was given special privileges, then later, they moved him to Berlin where he taught girls to speak on the propaganda radio programme.

When I heard about him he had been put on trial at Nuremberg and sent to prison. I wonder where he is now. He should have been shot for treason.

I've never really settled down. I had to start educating myself when I got into the army after returning to Jersey.

*Tommy Syms' birth certificate copied in 1942
to protect Tommy by proving he was of English Christian parentage, just
before he was deported to Birchenau .
See Tommy Syms' testimony.*

BIBERACH:
Tommy Syms was sent here from Jersey at the age of 10. He spent three years in this camp from 1942 to 1945.

EXTRACTED FROM THE BLACK BOOK

(SONDERFAHNDUNGSLISTE G.B.

150 people in alphabetical order of the 2820 listed in the infamous Black Book who would have been arrested, imprisoned and no doubt executed had the Germans won the war.

A.

14. Acland, Richard.
21. Adler, Friedrich, Dr.
39. Mac-Alpine, Charles B.
51. Angell, Normann.
67. Arnold-Forster, William Edward.
77. Astor, John.
77a. Astor, Lady.
79. Atholl, Duchess of, Katharine.
80. Attlee, Clement Richard.
81. Attlee, Clemens.

B.

6. Baden-Powell, Lord.
16. Baker-Noel, Philipp, J.
20. Ballantyne, Horatio.
43. Bartlett, Vernon Werner.
65. **Beaverbrook, Lord.**
75. Becker, Jerome Sidney.
98. Benes, Eduard, Dr. phil.
99. Benes, Vlcek, Hanna.
107. Bergh, van den, Clive.
108. Bergh, van den, Albert.
109. Bergh, van den, James Paul.
112. Bergh, van den, Sidney.
113. Bergh, van den Sam.
131. Bevin, Ernest.
145. Birkett, W.E.
182. Bonham-Carter, Lady, Violet.
188. Boothby, Robert.
199. **Bracken, Brendan.**
204. Brailsford, Henry Noel.

227. Brittain, Vera
265. Burnham, William Lawson

C.

2. Cadbury, Elizabeth
9. Camrose, Lord William E. Berry
19. Carter-Bonham, Asquith, Violet
29. Catlin, George Edward Cordon
31. Cazalet, Victor Alexander
33. Cecil, Lord, Robert
37. **Chamberlain, (Arthur) Neville)**
39. Chapman, Sir, Sidney John
49. **Churchill, Winston Spencer**
55. Citrine, Sir, Walter
64. Clavering, Sir, Albert
88. Cooper, Alfred, Duff.
96. Coward, Noel.
103. Cripps, Sir Stafford.
106. Crossfield, B.F.
107. Crossman, R.H.S.
108. Crowther, Goffrey.
111. Cunard, Nancy.

D.

20. Davies, David, Lord.
27. Dawson of Penn, Lord.
33. Delmer, Sefton.
79. Dodds, Eric Robertson.
105. Drummond, Lord.
114. Duff-Cooper, Alfred.
121. Duncan, Oliver, Sir.
122. Dunkan-Sendys.
132. Dutt, Palme, R.

69.	Lord Cademan of Silverdale, John.	59.	Trevelyan. Sir, Charles.
74.	Simon, Sir John Allsebrook.		**U.**
85.	Sinclair, Sir Archibald.	10.	Ustinov, (Middelton-Peddelton).
102.	Smallbones, Robert Tawnsen.		
124.	Snow, C.P.		**V.**
137.	Sorensen, Reginald William	6.	Vansittart, Robert.
140.	Southwood, Julius Salter Elias.		**W.**
2.	Spears, Edward Luis		
5.	Stanislawski, Jan.	63.	West, Rebecca
12.	Steed, Wikham.	10.	Walker-Smith, Sir, Jonah.
		53.	Weizmann, Chaim.
	T.	70.	White-Baker, John.
25.	Thorndike, Sybil.	116.	Woolf, Virginia.
27.	Thorton, James.		
55.	Trenchard, Barnett Herts. Lord Marshal		

Note:

The fact that the great appeasers, Halifax and Chamberlain are listed in The Black Book can only be interpreted as an expression of the compiler's opinion of those two men. A contemptuous gesture towards two weak, ineffective men who would have been of no use to the Germans as collaborators, therefore they were expendable.

On the other hand, if you were a collaborator with influence and a genuine believer in the Nazi articles of faith, such as Oswald Mosley, Lord Rothermere or even Captain Maule Ramsey, you would be used... and might even survive for a time as a puppet.

From AUSCHWITZ to ALDERNEY

BIBLIOGRAPHY

Recommended Reading
in association with this book

about Hitler, Germany, The Nazis and The Third Reich.

Mein Kampf.	: Adolf Hitler	
Life in the Third Reich.	: Edited by Richard Bessel Oxford	
	University Press	1987
Hitler	: A study in Tyranny.	
	: Alan Bullock. Penguin	1983
Hitler	: A Study in Personality and Politics	
	: William Carr	1978
	Edward Arnold	1988
Hitler.	: Joachim C. Fest Weidenfeld &	
	Nicholson	1974
The face of the Third Reich.	: Joachim C. Fest	1963
	Penguin	1988
The Holocaust.	: Martin Gilbert	
	Board of Deputies of British Jews	1978
The Meaning of Hitler.	: Sebastian Haffner	1979
	Weidenfeld & Nicholson	1988
Germany.	: Simon Taylor	1983
	Duckworth	1986
Adolf Hitler.	: John Toland	1976
	Ballantine	1987
Hitler's War Directives 1939/1945.		
	: Edited by H.R. Trevor-Roper	1964
	Pan Books	1978
The Last Days of Hitler.	: H.R. Trevor-Roper	1947
	Pan Books	1972

Last Waltz in Vienna.　　: George Clare
　　　　　　　　　　　　published in Germany　　　1980
　　　　　　　　　　　　published in G.B. by Macmillan
　　　　　　　　　　　　London Ltd
　　　　　　　　　　　　then by Pan Books Ltd.　　1981
Operation Sea Lion : German Plans for the invasion of England
　　1939 – 1942　　　　: Ronald Wheatley Clarendon Press1958

Recommended Reading
in association with this book

about The Nazi occupation of the Channel Islands, 1940 to 1945.

Isolated Island.　　　　: V.F Cortvriend　　　　　1947
　　　　　　　　　　　　Guernsey Star & Gasette 1949
The German Occupation of the Channel Islands :
　　　　　　　　　　　　Dr. Charles Cruickshank.
　　　　　　　　　　　　Alan Sutton　　　　　　1990
　　　　　　　　　　　　Oxford University Press　1975
Islands in Danger.　　　: Alan and Mary Wood　　1955
　　　　　　　　　　　　Four Square　　　　　　1967
The Alderney Story　1939/1949.
　　　　　　　　　　　　: St. J.M. Packe & Dreyfus M.
　　　　　　　　　　　　Alderney　　　　　　　1971
Jersey Under the Jackboot.　: R.C.F. Maughan CBE　　1946
　　　　　　　　　　　　W.H. Allen　　　　　　1964
The Silent War.　　　　: Frank Falla Burbridge Ltd　1967
　　　　　　　　　　　　reprints up to　　　　　1991
Hitler's Fortress Islands　　: Carel Toms
Germany's Occupation of the Channel Islands.
　　　　　　　　　　　　: New English Library
Seduction of a Nation (Leaflet)
　　　　　　　　　　　　: Thames Television Screen Guides 1989
German Tunnels in the Channel Islands
　　　　　　　　　　　　: Archives Book No. 7 by Michael
　　　　　　　　　　　　Ginns; plans by Paul Burnal
　　　　　　　　　　　　: Hawksworth Graphics & Print Ltd1994

Blueprints of Genocide   : Producer - Isabelle Rosin
                              Text adapted from BBC 2 programme
                              transmitted 9th May 1994.

The Model Occupation   : Madeline Bunting   1995
The Channel Islands under German Rule 1940 – 1945.
                              : Harper Collins   1995
The Channel Island War 1940 - 1945.
                              : Peter King   1991
                              Robert Hale/London
A file available from the Imperial War Museum Library, under REF:
     2726

A list of books concerned largely with
World War II Concentration Camps.

Auschwitz Trials   : E Bonhoeffer (1964-65)   1969   61p
                             Letters from an Eyewitness.

The Way Back   : The story of Lt. Cdr. Pat O'Leary.
                             (Mauthausen, Natzweiler & Dachau)
                             xii   1957 267p

The Spirit in the Cage   : Churchill Capt. P.   1954 251p
                             (Sachsenhausen)

The Real Enemy   : P D'Harcourt.   1967 vi 186p
                             (Buchenwald)

Licensed Massed Murder   : H. V. Dicks   1972   283p
                             a socio-pyschological study of some SS
                             killers.

The Holocaust Kingdom   : A Donat   1965 vi 361p
                             Maidanek and Dachau.

Hitler's SS.   : R Grunberger   1970   128p
The Liberation of Dachau April 29th 1945.
The Survivors : the story of the Belsen remnant.   1958 113p
Commandant of Auschwitz : the autobiography of Rudolf Hoess.
                                                     1959   252p
The Order of the Death's Head : the story of Hitler's SS xii
                                                     1969   690p
Anatomy of the SS State.   : H Krausnick & others. xvi 1968 614p
Mauthausen : the history of a death camp : E. Le Chene 1971 296p

SS and Gestapo : rule by terror. : R Manvell   1970   160p
The Incomparable Crime : Mass extermination in the twentieth
    century, the legacy of guilt. : R. Manvell and H. Fraenkel.
                                              1967 x   339p
Carve her name with Pride : a biography of Violette Szabo GC
    (Ravensbruck).   : R.J. Minney xii   1956   187p
Auschwitz : a report on the proceedings against Robert R. L. Hulka
    and others at Frankfort. : B. Naumann   1966   434p
Ashes in the Wind : the destruction of Dutch Jewry.
                              : J Presser   1965   556p
The Final Solution : The attempt to exterminate the Jews in Europe
    1939 – 1945.   1968   668p
No Banners : the story of Alfred and Henry Newton, Buchenwald.
                              : J. Thomas.   1955   340p
Odette : The story of a British Agent (Ravensbruck)   1955   286p
Wiener Library : Catalogue Series No. 1 – Persecution and resistence
    under the Nazis. 2nd Ed.   1960   208p
No Drums.. No Trumpets : The story of Mary Lindell Ravensbruck.
                              : B Wynne   1961   278p

OTHER RECOMMENDED READING.

Eminent Churchillians.   : Andrew Roberts Wiedenfeld &
                              Nicholson   1994
Life Sentence : The Memoirs of Lord Shawcross
                              Lord Shawcross. Constable £ 20 1995
The One that Got Away.   : Chris Ryan Century £ 14.99   1995
Fascism : A History.   : Roger Eatwell Chatto £ 20   1995
Fascism.   : Edited by Roger Griffin   1995
                              OUP £ 9.99
***Why the Allies Won.   : Richard Overy Cape £ 20   1995
    ***strongly recommended.
Eva's Story : A survivor's tale by the Step-sister of Anne Frank,
    Eva Schloss. Evelyn Julia Kent
                              ISBN 0/9518865   1994
The Disappearance of : Gina Schwarzmann, Goldie Rapaport,
    and Evelyn Julia Kent   ISBN 0/9523716/2/6

NOTES, REFERENCES AND SOURCES

read, used or viewed.

*Many of the items listed were read or viewed to provide the
Author with the background and feel of the subject on which to
build the book.

Many have not been used in the book ...

Acknowledgements are made to those sources where
information identifies.

In many cases where books cover a particular subject but
approach from a different direction it is natural the same
names and subject matter are repeated. For simplicity such
names have been grouped once only under the sub-heading.

Institutions

Files and Records

The Public Records Office

The Letters and Hansard: Parliamentary copyright
acknowledged, The House of Commons, SW1A

The Ministry of Defence: Crown copyright / MOD
acknowledged. Reproduced with the permission of the
Controller of HMSO.

Ministry of Defence, Whitehall Library, W1. 3/5 Gt. Scotland
Yard.

Ministry of Defence (Parliamentary Under Secretary of State
for Defence) Booklist No.2726

Files and Books consulted:

Imperial War Museum Library SE1/6HZ

The Black Book:

Imperial War Museum Library

Files and Books consulted:

The British Museum Library

Information:

The Old Bailey - London.

Senior Treasury Counsel.

Information:

The Bailiff of Jersey, C.I.

The Bailiff's Chambers.

Jean Claude Pressac's Book and others

The Institute of Contemporary History and The Wiener Library Ltd. London, W1.

Information:

The Auschwitz Museum via The Polish Embassy, London, W1.

The Russian Committee for Cinematography, 7 Malyi Gnezdnikovsky, Pereulok, Moscow, Russia.

Bundersarchiv, Abteilungen, Potsdam.

The Chief Executive of The Board of Deputies of British Jews, London, WC1H.

The Berlin Document Centre, Wasserk ferst g 1. 14163, Berlin.

German Tunnels in the Channel Islands.

The Channel Island Occupation Society (Jersey). Secty: W.M. Ginns, St. Ouen, Jersey, Channel Islands.

The Leaflet

The German Military Underground Hospital (The Custodian) La Vassalarie, St. Andrews, Guernsey, Channel Islands.

Leaflets, Book Extracts, Diary extracts.

Ann Corkett Griffiths of Bangor, Gwynedd, North Wales and of Guernsey. C.I.

Books

Encyclopedias and other reference books : Whittaker's Almanac : Churchill's 'History of the Second World War'

MEIN KAMPF

Psychological studies of Hitler, the Nazis and the Germans

Guernsey under German Rule :

Ralph Durand

Leaflet : FUHRER - Seduction of a Nation :

Covering ITV programme Thames International.

History of Philosophy :

(Character Study)

Dagobert D. Runes

Philosophical Library Inc.

New York. USA.

The Last Days of Hitler :

H. R. Trevor-Roper

Hitler's War Directives 1939-1945 :

H. R. Trevor-Roper

The Messianic Legacy :

Michael Baigent, Richard Leigh and Henry Lincoln.

Political Interests : referring to ***

*** The Changing Anatomy of Britain : Anthony Sampson

*** Their Trade is Treachery : Chapman Pincher

*** Traitors : Spies : Chapman Pincher

*** The British Connection : Russia's manipulation of British individuals and Institutions : Richard Deacon

*** The Climate of Treason : Spies : Andrew Boyle

*** Publish and be Damned : (Story of The Daily Mirror) : Hugh Cudlipp

Oswald Mosley : A heavily detailed historical biography of a remarkable man and his influence on pre-war political thinking : Robert Skidelsky

*** Winston Churchill; Beaverbrook; Hitler; Communism; Oswald Mosley; Duke of Windsor; M15; Chamberlain; National Front, Ant-semitism, Hore-Belisha..... John Strachey, the 5 spies, Hollis.

Subject : Auschwitz, the Holocaust and Extermination Camps

'Auschwitz' : techniques and operation of the gaschamber. : by Jean-Claude Pressac The Beate Klarsfield Foundation 1989

'Last Waltz in Vienna' The disintegration of a Jewish Family. : George Clare

'Eva's Story' : A survivor's tale by the step-sister of Anne Frank. : Eva Schloss with Evelyn Julia Kent

'And the Violins stopped Playing' : The story of Polish Gypsies escaping the holocaust to Hungary. : Alexander Ramati

'Anatomy of the Auschwitz Death Camp' (1994) : Israel Gulman

'The Holocaust' The Jewish Tragedy : Martin Gilbert

'After the Holocaust' : Martin Gilbert

'Hitler and the Final Solution' : Gerald Fleming

'Autobiography of Rudolf F F Hoess Commandant of Auschwitz : Rudolf F F Hoess

'The Nazi Doctors' : medical killing and the psychology of genocide. : Lifton/Robert Jay

General

'Eminent Churchillians' : Andrew Roberts

'Churchill' : A study in Failure : Sir Robert Rhodes James

'Fascism' : Edited by Roger Griffin

'Fascism' A history : Roger Eatwell

'Why the Allies Won' *** : Richard Overy

'THE BLACK BOOK' (Sonderfahndungaliste GB) List of 2820 British notables drawn up by the SS and discovered by British Army Intelligence in 1945. Also lists Union HQs., Freemason's Lodges, Universities etc. : Imperial War Museum Department of Printed Books 1989

Books about the Nazi Occupation of the Channel Islands

The German Occupation of the Channel Islands (The officially commissioned history) : Dr Charles Cruickshank

'The Channel Islands War 1940/1945' ** : Peter King

'German Tunnels in the Channel Isles' ** : by Michael Ginns with plans by Paul Burnal. Archive Book No.7 issued by the Channel Islands Occupation Society.

** Recommended reading

'Guernsey under German Rule' : Ralph Durand

'Islands in Danger' : Alan Wood and Mary Seaton Wood

'The Silent War' : Frank Falla

'Isolated Island' : V.V. Cortvriend (Mrs)

'Jersey under the Jackboot' : R.C.F. Maugham CBE

'The Diary' : Julia Tremayne (Mrs)

'A Peep behind the Screens' (memoirs of a nurse in Guernsey from 1940/1945) : Beryl S. Ozanne

'Five years of Fighting to Live' extracts from a diary kept by Mrs. Corkett who lived in Guernsey 1940/1945 and loaned to her daughter Mrs Ann Corkett Griffiths. : Mrs. Corkett Griffiths

Leaflet : Issued by permission of The Custodian of the German Military Underground Hospital.

'Hitler's Fortress Islands' (A pictorial record of the Occupation) : Carel Toms

Newspaper and Magazines (in alphabetical order)

The Daily Express
The Daily Telegraph
The Guardian
The Independent
The Independent on Sunday
The Liverpool Daily Post
The Mail on Sunday

The Sunday Express
The Sunday Observer
The Sunday Times
The Telegraph Magazine
The Times
The Times Book Review

The Times Literary   Time
  Supplement   The Spectator

Television programmes viewed

Granada, Feb 5th 1994
  Sidney Bernstein's Holocaust Film 'A painful reminder'
BBC 2 Richard Dimbleby: remembers his visit to Belsen in 1945.
BBC 2 10th May 1993
  Horizon - 'Blueprints of Genocide'
BBC 2 17th Nov 1994
  'Forbidden Britain' Riots and Mosley's Blackshirts
BBC 2
  'Hitler's Secret Weapon' Timewatch
BBC 2 The World at War'
  Dunkirk/Allied advance into Europe/Genocide/
  American Nazi Party/Americans and the Japs/Bomber
  Harris/America and N. Africa/Holland/etc
Granada
  'Reputations' Pope Pius XII World War 2 and the Nazis.
Granada, 21st Feb. 95, 'Combat 18'
BBC 2, 1995
  'Plea for a UK Holocaust Museum' by Dr David Cesarani
BBC 2, 1995
  'Churchill's Wartime speeches
BBC 2, 1995
  'The French Holocaust'
BBC 2, 1995
  'Hitler's death' and 'V2 bombing of London' (two
  programmes)
BBC 2, 1995
  'The Churchills'
BBC 2, 20th June 1995
  'Myths and Memories of World War 2'